This book is dedicated . . .

to my parents, who were always hospitable and made home a welcoming place;

to my twin aunts, Lor and Helen, whose home was always in order and full of joy;

to our young adult children, Mark, Lisa, and Christy (and her husband Brian),
who are establishing homes of their own;

to my husband, David, who has supported me and our changing
household over the years;

to all the men who support the changing roles of the women in their lives—whether
mother, sister, or wife—and the home reflected by it;

to women who truly want order and freedom for the spaces they live and work in;

and to you, my new friend, as we walk side by side to simplify
the spaces in your home.

Change your home—change your space—change your life!

Contents

Simplify Your Storage Space

1

Simply Start Out Right

With a good organizational plan, you can be sure to unclutter any area
of your home. And if you maintain the neat, orderly space you've created,
you'll always know what you've got—and exactly where to find it.

—MERVYN KAUFMAN

love the look of a clean home—and you probably do too. But wanting an orderly home and actually bringing it about are two different things. If you sometimes struggle to maintain your space, you're not alone. Most of us eventually have to admit, "I just have too much *stuff*!"

I, too, didn't realize the clutter I had collected until I opened my linen closet years ago and found *twenty-six* tablecloths. That's enough for a new one every two weeks for an entire year! That day I discovered what too much felt like. So I started to sort and create simple solutions to control clutter.

As we all know, cluttered closets (like my overstuffed linen closet), paper pileups, and overflowing countertops gradually fill our homes for a variety of reasons, ranging from a busy schedule to other people to pick up after. Then, adding to our piles of stuff, we receive gifts, find great bargains, and purchase new things to enjoy without getting rid of the old. Before long, the clutter grows in every room and we feel out of control!

If we don't simplify the things we own, our homes become full of gathered belongings and we become "museum" keepers. And the more things we acquire, the more time we have to spend taking care of them. Without an effective system to organize our belongings, we spend many frustrating hours searching for important things that are lost or misplaced.

Put quite simply, too much stuff complicates our lives.

Get Things Back Under Control

Perhaps things have gotten a bit cluttered in your life. If so, let me assure you that having too much stuff is not a character flaw! It can be the sign of a busy life, a sentimental attachment to things, indecisiveness, or reluctance to let things go. Whatever the reason, in this book you will learn practical tips to help you overcome your past and make a fresh start.

There are simple solutions to getting things back under control. You don't have to live in a complicated home. You can make changes . . . at your own pace. The dream of a simplified space can become your reality.

The good news is that when you simplify your belongings, you will find not only clear space but also more time. You won't be taking care of so many things, and that will free you to focus on what really matters. Now is the time to let things go, for your benefit and for others'.

Motivated to Change

We all have personal reasons for wanting to simplify our space. Mine was embarrassment.

My well-organized twin aunts were visiting from out of town for a week. I loved my aunts and knew they were neat as a pin at home and work. Thinking I could use a little encouragement from them on how to get organized, I casually asked as we were setting the table for dinner, "Aunt Helen, how can I get these papers on my kitchen counter in order?"

She folded her arms, took a step back, and surveyed the situation. I knew right then I was in trouble. Sure enough, Aunt Helen began to assess my situation aloud.

"First of all, you need to get rid of these piles on the countertop. Then the piles sitting on the floor underneath the counter need to go. And then . . ."

As she continued, I was mortified. I thought, *Can't she see I'm a busy person? I'm raising a family with three kids! What does she expect?*

I started to blame my family for my disorganized lifestyle, but it wasn't their fault. The fact remained: I had a cluttered kitchen, and I was responsible. What I had visually tuned out as a minor problem was a noticeable eyesore to everyone else. I decided to change.

Make a Plan and Take Some Action Every Day

You may not have an Aunt Helen in your life, but you may have heard comments from a spouse, neighbor, or friends (or feared getting some). This may be your moment to do some clearing out and cleaning up. If not for others, then do it for yourself. The peace of mind is well worth it.

Here's what I learned as I pursued organizing my paper-filled countertop:

1. Keeping things out is the slowest way to find anything. It all runs together and is difficult to find anything, from the credit card bill to the coupon for a favorite store.
2. Getting organized is only half the battle. I had to go a step further and prioritize things to keep and things to let go.
3. Living an organized lifestyle is much easier than living a disorganized one. No one told me it was way more fun and took much less time. Once I discovered this secret, I was hooked on keeping a simplified space, and you probably will be too.

Little did I know back then I would not only clean up my space, but I would encourage audiences and clients across the country with the hope that they too could make changes. Orderliness is not a gene you are born with; anyone can learn to sort, organize, and simplify successfully—starting today!

How Do You Simplify Your Space?

Simplifying your space is the process of organizing your belongings and letting go of the excess until your surroundings are orderly and peaceful. We're going to do it room by room so you can see your progress.

As you simplify your space, you might be doing one of several things. For instance, you might be clearing up a cluttered coffee table by separating paper from other items. Or you might be going through a closet and donating a good portion of the contents to charity. Or you might be making room in the garage by organizing sections and getting rid of excess clutter.

Think of the process like a pyramid. *Sorting* is the base, *organizing* is the next block, and *simplifying* your space is the attractive pyramid point that shows you have completed the space.

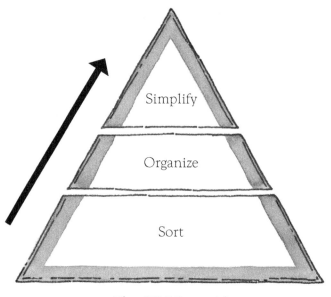

Simplify

Organize

Sort

The SOS Pyramid

 SPACE-SAVING TIP #1

To simplify your space, you *sort* things to give away, *organize* the remaining items, and then *simplify* by neatly arranging your favorites.

How Are We Going to Do This?

Simplify Your Space takes you through your home in a way that will give you the biggest results in the least amount of time. The book's easy-to-follow sequence covers your entire home from the most visible and used spaces to the larger and less used storage areas.

Simplify Your Visible Space
Kitchen—Family Room—Daily Paperwork

Simplify Your Personal Space
Bedroom—Bedroom Closet—Bathroom

Simplify Your Active Space
Laundry Room—Child's Room—Office

Simplify Your Formal Space
Dining Room—Living Room—Guest Room

Simplify Your Storage Space
Garage—Basement—Your Next Move

Simply Maintain and Multiply Your Success

The sections of this book, as well as the three chapters in each section, progress from easier to more challenging rooms. You don't want to get lost organizing a back closet when your family room media center is screaming for attention. Simplify the things in your home that are the most visible first, and then organize the less used rooms last, which need your finely tuned skills to work up to them.

I drop organizing hints in each chapter (fifty-two throughout the book), so you can follow the chapter sequence or you can go to the room chapter of your choice. Passion to start and finish a job creates momentum, and that's what we're looking for!

By following the step-by-step directions in each chapter, you will be equipped to succeed. Living in a clean, organized home creates a sense of serenity and order. You'll feel good about yourself and your space.

Ready, Set, Go!

Read each chapter, follow the strategies and tips that work for you, and then stand at the door of the room with that chapter's checklist in hand. Success means many "yeses" on the checklist at the end of each chapter or when you clean up what you started for the day.

Too often, inexperienced people start to organize without a specific plan and end up making a bigger mess than when they started. No more! To ensure you won't end up creating more piles in a helter-skelter sorting frenzy, in each room we will follow my CALM approach, an easy acronym to remember that will keep you focused.

CREATE A PLAN
APPROACH IT BY SECTIONS
LIGHTEN UP AND LET GO
MANAGE IT SIMPLY

Think of me as your personal organizer, coaching you through each room of your house. You will be able to see *and* feel the organized approach to each room. I think you can do this yourself, but if you have trouble making decisions you may want to invite a friend to join you.

This process may take one day or one week per room, depending on the amount accumulated and how determined you are to create a simplified space. The problems multiply the more they sit there. But the more you overcome them, the more skilled you will become.

By the end of the book, you will be problem solving like an organizing pro as you personalize these systems. One drawer, one cabinet, and one countertop at a time, you can simplify your space.

You Can Do This!

There is a Finnish proverb that says, "Happiness is a place between too little and too much." We are going to find that place—the place where you are content with what you have and not overwhelmed by having too much.

Then the fun begins when you can decorate and put your personal touches in each room. To help you do that, I've invited restaging and interior design expert Susan Wells to provide decorating tips in each chapter.

Think of the benefits of a simplified home: No more endless searching for items you need. No more rummaging through drawers, cabinets, and shelves for lost or misplaced items. Things will now have a designated space in your home so they will be right where you need them when you want them. The benefits will multiply the more you simplify.

So whenever you see a pile of clutter that looks daunting, remind yourself to break it down to one section at a time and declare, "That's not hard. Even I can do this!"

I say this not just from my experience as a professional organizer but from my own personal experience. As I put the finishing touches on this book, we moved across country from San Diego to Dallas. My message was especially put to the test as we moved to a smaller home—one less bedroom, one less bathroom, and one less garage space. Consolidating and simplifying our belongings took some time and effort, but the result was an organized move into a neatly arranged home.

Change your space—change your home—change your life. A new life of order and freedom awaits you. Soon you will see your home in a new light and with clear spaces. Enjoy the journey!

Ten Tips to Simplify Any Space

You can begin to simplify any space with these ten easy tips:

1. Keep the front two-thirds of every countertop (or desk) clear.
2. Do a two-minute pickup before you leave a room.
3. Put clothes away now rather than later.
4. Make your clean kitchen table a focal point with only a centerpiece.
5. Look for a clear line of sight in every room.
6. Open your mail in one spot with five key file folders.
7. Create a file for recurring papers in your life.
8. Organize one shelf, file, or drawer at a time.
9. Continue to pare things down until you can manage them.
10. Congratulate yourself on living space you maintain daily.

Remember, one pile sitting out is the potential beginning of a complicated life.
Keep your life simple, and put the pile away.

—MARCIA RAMSLAND

Simplify Your Visible Space

Let's begin with the three most used and visible spaces in your home: the kitchen, the family room, and the daily paperwork spot. Once you see these three spaces clean every day, you'll gain the confidence to conquer the rest of your home! After all, you get to practice on these rooms daily.

2

Simplify Your Kitchen

In most homes, the kitchen is the hub—the one room where friends and family gather regularly to prepare meals, exchange stories, and catch up on the day's events. So why not make it an efficient workspace and an inviting place to hang out?

—JOANNE KELLAR BOUKNIGHT AND JOHN LOECKE

Can you think of the best conversation you ever had in a kitchen—at a friend's home, your grandmother's house, or around your childhood kitchen table? Chances are there was a comfortable chair to sit in, an inviting aroma coming out of the oven, and someone who took the time to talk with you. Yet in many kitchens today, there are piles of paper to move to get to that chair, dirty dishes piled in the sink, and a frantic rush to figure out the answer to the ever-popular question: "What's for dinner tonight?"

Many of us have such busy schedules that we lack the time to make our kitchen and meals live up to our expectations. But with a plan to simplify the space, your kitchen can become a place of warmth and welcome. After all, it's likely the most used room in your house when people are home.

Create a Plan

The most important part of simplifying your space is to follow a plan so you know where to begin and where you left off.

To simplify your kitchen, start with your countertops and kitchen table. When your countertops and table are clean, you can walk into your kitchen and have a clear line of sight. Resist the temptation to store excess items on your countertops. Everything needs a place in your kitchen space!

After you've followed the steps for a clear line of sight in your kitchen, then you can sort the less visible spaces, such as drawers, cabinets, and the pantry.

Simplify Your Kitchen

Motivation:
- I want my kitchen to look nice all the time.
- I want cooking and cleanup to be easier.
- I want to have room in my kitchen for my family to help cook.

Supplies:
- Wastebasket and recycle bin for items to be discarded
- Donation box for items to be given away
- "Put Away" box for items that belong in other rooms

Time Estimate:
4–6 hours (approximately 15 minutes per drawer or shelf)

Reward:
An organized kitchen that looks nice and is ready to use anytime.

The kitchen is made up of many small spaces, so it is easy to get lost on rabbit trails trying to put things away. To overcome this, select one wall to focus on each day. That way, you will know where to start and stop.

It's also easy to clean up a drawer or shelf as you're putting away the dinner dishes. This way, you gradually accumulate completed spaces, which encourages you to complete the room.

Approach It by Sections

Follow these steps with an eye on the clock. Estimate how long each step will take and then see if you can stick to it or move along more quickly. If you get stuck on where an item should go, put it in a "maybe" box to decide at the end of the room sort. You will get better at decision making the more you do it.

Sink

Start with a clean sink by washing and putting away dirty dishes and recent clutter. It may take you about thirty minutes to clear the table, load the dishwasher, and clean the sink. Then commit to washing and putting away dishes after each meal to keep your kitchen sink clutter at bay.

Table

A clean kitchen table can set the tone for your entire home. It is one of the most used gathering spots and should be ready for action anytime.

A simple way to keep your kitchen table looking nice is to keep it cleared except for a tasteful centerpiece. Then it always looks nice whether you are walking by for a drink of water, helping the kids do their homework, or chatting with a neighbor over a cup of coffee. If you keep up on nothing else in your home, keep your kitchen table cleared off and something of interest, such as a silk flower arrangement, as a centerpiece.

Countertops

Pull everything forward and wash each counter and item. Put back only the things you like and use regularly. Place the remaining items in a donation box or wastebasket. Once the front two-thirds of your counters and the top of your kitchen table are clear, the line of sight into your kitchen is clean. This is the key to making your kitchen look clean: keep the countertops and table clear of daily clutter.

SPACE-SAVING TIP #2

Keep your kitchen clean by maintaining a clear line of sight on your table and the front two-thirds of your countertops.

Floor

A clean floor is the second most important visual level for a kitchen after the countertops and table. It's time to sweep up the crumbs and wash the floor to keep this very large surface clean. People do notice your floors.

It's wise to determine how often you need to clean the floor to keep it looking nice: does it need to be part of your nightly cleanup routine, once a week, or once every two weeks? The answer depends on the number of people, pets, and traffic in and out of your kitchen. The more often the room is used, the more often you have to clean it. Plus, the rest of your home will be cleaner if people don't track kitchen dirt into the rest of the house!

Refrigerator

The most clutter in your kitchen is often found on the biggest item in your kitchen—the refrigerator. "Visual tune out" keeps most homeowners from noticing the actual clutter on the door front and on top of the refrigerator.

Take everything off the front of your refrigerator and put magnets on a less visible side. Make it attractive: a grocery list and pen on the side, a magnet for each child's work on the front, and favorite pictures on the top one-third of the refrigerator doors.

What do you do with the other papers on your refrigerator? Place coupons in a coupon holder in a drawer, photos in a photo album on the coffee table, children's papers in three-ring memory books in the family room, sales fliers and invitations in a file near your monthly calendar, and phone numbers from magnets in your telephone book.

The top of the refrigerator is best used as a decorative shelf with a silk plant and nice display, not as storage for appliances or food boxes.

SPACE-SAVING TIP #3

Reduce kitchen cleanup time by placing dirty dishes in the dishwasher, returning foods to the refrigerator, and putting countertop items back in cabinets within ten minutes after each meal.

Now that the visible space is clean, you can tackle the "invisible spaces" in your kitchen, such as drawers, cabinets, and the pantry. Move from smaller to larger invisible

1. Clear Table and Countertops
2. Organize All Lower Cabinets
3. Organize All Upper Cabinets

surfaces. The smaller the contained space (like a drawer or a shelf), the more manage-able it is to conquer. Let's place our three sorting tools (wastebasket, donation box, and "put away" box) next to the area you are organizing.

Drawers

Begin with one drawer at a time, and work from top to bottom in one section. Organize the most used drawers first, such as silverware, cooking utensils, plastic wrap, measuring cups, and so on.

The smaller the items, the shallower the drawer they should be in. Often you will have a drawer with silverware and serving utensils, another with cooking utensils, and another with plastic-wrap boxes lined up side by side.

Be sure to use drawer dividers to keep your particular setup from sliding around. You can do this by measuring the drawer and making a diagram to take with you to the store to select mesh or plastic dividers. Or you can use gift box lids to organize the contents of your drawers.

- Empty one drawer, wipe it out, and use dividers to keep items from sliding around.
- The most used items go in the front one-third of the drawer, the middle section holds the next most used items, and the back holds storage.
- Toss the clutter and donate unused items.
- Keep only what you like and use.
- Keep the drawer simple and visually pleasing.

SPACE-SAVING TIP #4

You can organize any drawer in three simple steps: empty everything, wipe it out, and replace only the contents you currently use.

Each drawer should fill two criteria. First, the drawer should have a "theme" (such as silverware or dishtowels) and be located near where the enclosed items are used. Keep it that way by putting a label on the inner edge of the drawer to remind others to maintain the order.

Second, drawers should only hold items that fit the size and location of the space. Store items vertically if possible so it is easy to see the contents, such as small appliances, cooking utensils, and perhaps even pots and lids. Again, store things near where they are used so everything is within easy reach.

Cabinets

Cabinets can make or break the function and simplicity of your kitchen. Just because items are behind closed doors doesn't mean they should be disorganized! Don't let useful items turn into clutter by overfilling the cabinets.

Clean the nearest countertop and then empty one shelf at a time. As you sort through each item in each cabinet, ask yourself, "Is this still part of my current cooking style, or should I pass it on to someone else?" Place items you definitely want to keep on your left, items you maybe want to keep in the middle, and items you want to donate or discard on the right.

When you have pared down a cabinet, replace the useful items with labels facing forward and the front three inches of every shelf empty to maintain a clean look.

Pantry

Your pantry can become overstuffed and useless if food items are difficult to locate or if unused kitchen items are stored there. To keep a simple kitchen, you will want to clean out your pantry just as often as you do your refrigerator.

Just because canned goods stored in the pantry have longer expiration dates than fresh foods in the refrigerator doesn't mean they can live beyond your careful scrutiny of how long you should keep them. Go through your pantry shelves regularly and ask yourself, "Do I like this food item, and do I still cook with it?" If so, plan a meal with it. If not, pass the excess items on to a mission or shelter that could use them.

Group food items together: canned soups, tomato sauces, and vegetables. Group jars together: pasta sauce, salsa, and jellies. Group bags of chips, pretzels, and dried fruit in containers together for snacks.

Lower shelving should hold the largest items, most used items in the middle, and smaller, lesser used foods on the top shelves. For a neat and clean look, label the shelves with a label maker or masking tape and pen: cereals, baking supplies, vegetables, soups, snacks, and so on. Leave the front three inches open so you and others can read the label and keep your system going.

If the system isn't working, adjust it until everyone knows where to put things away.

Trash

Clean homes have one thing in common: empty wastebaskets. Empty wastebaskets show attention to detail and make others more likely to throw their trash away! That means less clutter in the house too.

Be sure to keep your trash can and recycle container clean. Wash them as needed.

Lighten Up and Let Go

Once you finish organizing for the day, take your donations to a charity, return items to their owners, and toss the clutter within twenty-four hours. Don't toss them into the back of your car or hold them in the garage for a spring time garage sale! Get them back into circulation now. This is often the hardest step—to get the sorted items out the door and off the premises.

- One client was surprised to find she had nine frying pans, including duplicates of every size. Now that she had grade-school children and was always on the run, omelets and crepes were not a part of her life. She simplified her kitchen space and gained more room by selecting three frying pans and passing on the rest to a charity.

- Another client organized her drawer of knives and found she had thirteen butcher-type knives from wedding present sets and free cooking demonstrations. She reclaimed an entire drawer by sending all but two off to a rescue mission kitchen.

- Mary had stemware in her kitchen cabinets that wasn't practical for her college-age children. Her daughter asked her to box it up and save it for her first apartment. Space saved? An entire cabinet shelf while the box was stored in a closet in the basement.

As a final step, stand at the entrance to your kitchen and use this checklist to appreciate your hard work and determine your next steps.

Kitchen Checklist

_____ 1. Is the kitchen sink empty and clean?

_____ 2. Are the front two-thirds of my counters clear, and the rest attractive and useful?

_____ 3. Is the kitchen table wiped off and clutter free?

_____ 4. Is the floor clean and washed?

_____ 5. Is the refrigerator door tidy, the top clean, and extra papers neatly filed?

_____ 6. Are the drawers organized with like items in dividers and easy to use?

_____ 7. Are items in cabinets pared down and the front three inches of every shelf empty?

_____ 8. Is my pantry clutter free and items easy to find?

_____ 9. Is my trash can emptied regularly before it overflows?

_____ 10. Am I pleased with how my kitchen looks and functions?

SPACE-SAVING TIP #5

If you can't go through the kitchen all in one day, then do a little each day while cleaning up after a meal.

Tips from "The Decorating Coach," Susan Wells

Create decorator touches out of eyesores in the kitchen with some ingenuity. Exchange a commercial container for a striking glass jar, and fill with a dish soap that complements your decor.

Create a simple theme above kitchen cabinets with generous, even spacing between groupings of similar objects (at least ten inches in height). Alternate sets of two or three rectangular baskets storing seasonal items. Accent the groupings with a vase or artificial greenery.

Who said that attractive tableware can't be functional? Start with pretty placemats. Keep salt and pepper in stylish shakers. Display fruit in an attractive bowl or wire basket. Upgrade from ho-hum plastic to glass serving bowls. Your tableware communicates how special every meal is together.

Manage It Simply

Once you have gone through every section of your kitchen, keep checking back to see that the drawers, cabinets, and pantry stay in order. Do a line-of-sight cleanup across the kitchen counters each day.

Here's an easy way you can simply manage your kitchen and keep it in great shape:

What?	When?
Sink, Countertops, and Table	Daily cleanup after meals
Floor	Daily cleanup after dinner
Cabinets and Drawers	Weekly maintenance
Refrigerator and Pantry	Daily tidy up one shelf and plan the next day's meals

Review: The CALM Kitchen Approach

Create a Plan
- Clear the sink, countertops, and table.
- Declutter the refrigerator door and pantry.
- Organize drawers and cabinets.

Approach It by Sections
- Arrange one shelf or drawer per day.
- Focus on one wall at a time.
- Schedule one big cleaning day to finish the kitchen.

Lighten Up and Let Go
- Charities such as the Salvation Army, AmVets, and the American Cancer Society appreciate donations and often provide free pickup service.
- Your friends and family may enjoy some of your unneeded items.
- Consider donating items to newlyweds, college kids, or others who could put them to good use.

Manage It Simply
Daily—Clear the "line of sight" on countertops, table, refrigerator door, and floor.
Weekly—Check one wall of drawers and cabinets.
Monthly—Review the contents of your pantry.

To simplify your kitchen space, begin with one small space at a time and keep going. Once you have simplified and organized the contents of your kitchen, this space will be much easier for your family to use and keep clean.

Think of your kitchen as a café, a gathering place for fun and conversation.
Food preparation is only one of the many functions of this room.
Walk into your kitchen and see it with fresh eyes.

—ALEXANDRA STODDARD

3

Simplify Your Family Room

Perhaps you call it the living room, or the family room, or the den. . . .
Ideally, these rooms should be comfortable and inviting, and
have ample space for relaxing with family and friends.

—MERYL STARR

The family room is the main room in your home for people to gather for conversation, relaxation, and entertainment. The family room can be an extended section of the kitchen, a room all its own, or a corner of another room.

Any way you look at it, the family room is the key gathering room in the house after the kitchen. How you set up and maintain this room can simplify or complicate the clutter at home.

One Family's Story

Julia and I had spent the morning clearing the visible space in her kitchen. The kitchen table was clean, and the front two-thirds of the countertops now had a clear line of sight. We had also spent an additional hour finding a home for every paper and unfinished project on her kitchen island until it was impressively clean.

As Julia raved about the beautiful, now visible space in her clean kitchen, we went to sit down in the adjacent family room. But we had to move piles of toys and reading materials off the couch. The family room had the same malady as the kitchen—no systems, no storage, and no daily pickup. It needed help!

"I'm so sorry about this," Julia said as she carted off a stack of kids' books. "It doesn't usually get this bad."

"Let's take a minute and talk about the family room," I followed up. "What activities happen here? Is your storage working for each activity?"

Instead of clearing the room in a helter-skelter fashion, we created a plan to set it up and make cleanup simple.

Create a Plan

Everyone in Julia's family used the family room, but no one felt responsible to clean it up. Hence the disarray of projects, homework, magazines, and toys strewn about.

Our plan started with cleaning the center of the room and then moving to the outer walls. The table-height surfaces were first to be cleared, then the floor, and then wall shelving and high surfaces. Going in a clockwise fashion one wall at a time keeps the system on track.

Decide the current uses of your family room by jotting down what it is used for this week. This could include:

- *Watch TV and movies.* You need all the DVDs stored together and a shelf by the back door to put ones to return.
- *Listen to music and read.* You need bookshelves and a storage holder that holds the CDs attractively.
- *A meeting room.* Perhaps you occasionally host large family gatherings or a neighborhood board meeting, so you need extra seating that can be removed when you are alone or just with your family.
- *An extra space for company.* In a nearby closet, store an air mattress and pillows for an occasional overnight guest or teen sleepover.

All these uses signal three functions of the family room: personal, family, and social. It is definitely an important room to keep improving to meet those changing needs.

Simplify Your Family Room

Motivation:

- ◘ I want to organize our media so I can find things easily.
- ◘ I want to enjoy my family room more.
- ◘ I've got to get ready for company!

Tools:

- ◘ Wastebasket and recycle bin for items to be discarded
- ◘ Donation box for items to be given away
- ◘ "Put Away" box for items that belong in other rooms

Time Estimate:

1–3 hours

Reward:

A family room that looks tidy and contains things that are easy to find.

Approach It by Sections

The main sections of the family room set the stage for simplifying the space: table-height surfaces followed by "centers" in the family room, such as entertainment center, bookshelves, and computer center. Learn to walk into any room and view the clear lines of sight in that same order.

Coffee Table and End Tables

The center of the family room is typically a coffee table or chest of some kind. Usually this table accumulates too much stuff, so clear it off and then decide what to put back. You may choose an orderly array of current magazines (no more than three), a decorative item, and a basket for the remote controls. Less is more on the coffee table, since it is the center of your visual attention at sitting height.

In Julia's family room, the end tables and counter-height chest were covered in reading piles, schoolbooks, or unfinished games. They evidenced a lot of activity but no cleanup—though these things should be put away the same day.

Your coffee table and end tables need a system. Clean them up before the next meal. You might consider making a quick family room checkup before dinner is served or the TV goes on.

SPACE-SAVING TIP #6

The sign of a good system is the rate of retrieval and return. The easier it is to find and return things, the more likely the system will stay intact.

CDs and DVDs

Once it was only paper that cluttered our family rooms. But now the piles consist of smaller, more expensive, and just as cluttering CDs and DVDs. Store these items close to where they are used. And to simplify the look, intentionally use holders or drawers that they can neatly line up in. If you are always adding to your collections, drawer space with dividers allows new titles to be placed alphabetically without having to move every CD in a slotted storage container.

TV and Accessories

Store your remote controls and TV guide in a basket on the coffee table, in the drawer of an end table, or tucked beside the TV in the entertainment center. Decide as a family where these items will go or they will become tabletop clutter you chase every day. If you decide together, everyone will be able to find them when their show is ready to start. The last person watching gets to put everything away.

Computer and Computer Accessories

Computers and computer accessories, such as mouse, keyboard, and monitor, are sometimes placed in the family room, especially if younger kids are using the Internet. If you have computers in the family room, make sure there is storage next to each computer for CDs and useful manuals, and a surface beside it to work. Find stylish storage baskets or file drawers so piles don't develop on or around the computer. For more information on organizing a computer desk, see chapter 10.

Magazines and Newspapers

Purchasing a magazine holder or designating a wicker basket for magazines and newspapers is the start of organization, but it's only half of the equation. You need a

1. Clear Table and Furniture Surfaces
2. Organize DVDs, CDs, Magazines
3. Organize Bookshelves

system determining how long you keep them. With magazines, newspapers, and catalogs, the most efficient system is "New one in, old one out" even if you have to read it on the spot! Otherwise, a magazine holder tidies up the paper clutter.

Bookshelves

Every book has value and can change your life, but decide when some books should come off your bookshelves to make room for new ones. Sort your books into a "keep" or "giveaway" pile yearly. Organize your books by categories and label the shelves to maintain order. Limit your collection to the size of your bookshelves by donating books to your public library.

SPACE-SAVING TIP #7

Anything piled up is a telltale sign that it is "homeless." Weed out your cabinets until you create a spot for it to belong.

Toys and Games

Toys and games can take over a family room quickly, so be sure to have shelving, cabinets, or bins that they can be returned to each day. Teach your children from a young age to have "cleanup time" before they leave the room. It can be as much fun as playing if everyone pitches in and tries to beat a kitchen timer.

Large toys go on the bottom shelves, books on the middle shelves, and small blocks or puzzles go on trays or in their boxes on the top shelves to be brought down when there is a clear space to play on. The specifics of toy storage depend on the ages of the children.

Lighten Up and Let Go

How do you know if you have too much of something, such as books, CDs, games, or toys? It comes down to what fits in your space and how it looks. If you are not using items and they overflow your designated area, pass them on.

Pull everything out of a section and then sort them into three categories:

* Keep
* Put Away Elsewhere
* Get Rid Of

Deliver these piles back to where they belong right away. Deliver charity items within twenty-four hours. That is the key to simplifying space—immediately deliver the items to finish the job!

If you own more things than you have space to store, you have only two choices: downscale the amount of items in a category or increase the storage space. I prefer to downscale first because it looks and functions better. And downscaling your items also frees up your valuable time.

You only have so many hours in a day and in your lifetime. So learn to recognize when a phase of your life is over—the record collection, the VHS collection, the children's books. Then replace it with the interests of your current lifestyle. Don't keep adding to what you have. You have to learn to subtract.

Family Room Checklist

_____ 1. Is the coffee table clutter free and attractive?

_____ 2. Are the end tables ready to use and piles gone?

_____ 3. Are the TV guide and remote put away but easy to access?

_____ 4. Are the DVDs and CDs in a drawer or container near where they are used?

_____ 5. Are toys sorted and neatly stored?

_____ 6. Are the bookshelves working for everyone who reads in the family room?

_____ 7. Are current magazines available and the old ones recycled?

_____ 8. Are catalogs out of sight but available?

_____ 9. Does the newspaper have a daily or weekly rotation cycle and look neat?

_____ 10. Is my family room the organized and comfortable room we call "home"?

Tips from "The Decorating Coach," Susan Wells

Bookshelves don't have to be boring. Give away paperbacks that you don't plan to read again. Remove the jackets of any clothbound books to reveal their rich texture and color.

Within their category, organize sets of four to six books by size or by complementary colors, such as red books, blue books, and brown books. Don't cram your books together—leave room to focus on the beauty of each collection.

Accent a grouping with a vase or pillar candle. Adorn the top of a stack of books with a family photo. The picture, frame, and matting should harmonize with the area. You can even recolor your photo matting with a touch of spray paint to make it look brand new! Finally, conceal papers and necessities in richly woven storage baskets artfully placed throughout the shelving.

Manage It Simply

There are two ways to manage your family room. One is by solving the overflow problems by sections until the excess is gone and the useful items are saved. The second way is to do a daily sweep through the family room and put things away before the next meal. Insist on cleanup before meals and before the TV goes on. This keeps the room from getting out of hand . . . and saves you a lot of time in the long run.

Remember, daily maintenance of a room is easier and takes less time than a major overhaul. Don't let a space deteriorate into a room full of unfinished project clutter.

- Jan loved having the latest magazines so she wouldn't miss anything. When we sorted the magazine piles on her coffee table, we ended up with seventeen magazines! She thought about all the time and money she would save with fewer subscriptions. In fact, she cut back to less than half of that. Her cluttered room—and mind—were much clearer from then on.

- Kate was storing her children's books neatly in cardboard boxes on the fireplace mantel. When we talked about how unattractive and temporary that was, she discovered a decorative yet unused cabinet that could hold the books and tossed the cardboard boxes.

- Don loved his sports and travel magazines but couldn't get his wife to appreciate that he needed a spot for them. Finally he went to an office supply store and bought leather magazine holders. He gave away some of his old textbooks to be able to place the magazines on the bookshelf.

With a few simple steps to clear the clutter spots and simplify the space, you can have an attractive and enjoyable family room. Solve each clutter problem one at a time, and you will simplify your family room section by section.

SPACE-SAVING TIP #8

Keep a clear line of sight across your coffee table, end tables, and couch to make the family room appear clean and ready all the time.

Review: The CALM Family Room Approach

Create a Plan
○ Start clearing and organizing table surfaces.
○ Organize and downscale one section at a time.
○ Look for ways to organize and finish projects sooner.

Approach It by Sections
○ Clear the table surfaces of clutter.
○ Organize and "containerize" your electronic media.
○ Store magazines in holders and store books on shelves with a good reading light next to your favorite chair.

Lighten Up and Let Go
○ Excess media can be given to charity or sold online.
○ Excess books can be donated to your library.
○ Excess magazines can be given to a hospital, doctor's office, or school.

Manage It Simply
Daily—Check the family room for pileups before dinnertime.
Weekly—Dust, vacuum, and clean your family room to keep it looking tidy.
Seasonally—Go through cabinets and shelves before school starts or before the holidays.

Learn to walk into the family room and put items away. You can do a lot of sorting during TV commercials, and then you never have to do a big cleanup!

Company is a great motivator to manage your space, so invite people over and enjoy your family room more!

Generally speaking, it's easier to remember where everything is if you store like items together.

—JOANNE KELLAR BOUKNIGHT AND JOHN LOECKE

4

Simplify Your Daily Paperwork

*The good news is that it is compelling to keep a workspace open,
once you have established a system for managing papers.
The bad news is that without a system, paper piles up.*

—PORTER KNIGHT

Cindy opened the door and welcomed me into her living room. "I'm so glad you're here," she said with relief. "My husband says I really need to get organized."

As we walked through her home, I noticed the living room was well decorated and neat as a pin. The family room was clean and clutter free, too, especially for a family with four children. Even the dining room and hallway bathroom were perfect. By the time we got to the kitchen, I wondered what the problem was . . . until I saw "IT."

Oh my. Now I know why I'm here, I reflected. We stood in the doorway facing an overflowing pile of papers to the right of the kitchen sink. The sea of papers covered the counter and was almost touching the cabinet above it.

Cindy's kitchen was the heart of her home—and it was the resting place for all her mail and paperwork. Her papers had accumulated on the counter by the telephone . . . and then spread out to the kitchen table and an unused chair. In this case, the daily mail pile and papers were a source of stress for her and her family.

Get Your Paperwork Under Control

Like so many client households, the piles of paper that accumulate in the kitchen demote the most used room in the house into a less than desirable place. Let's face it, undone paperwork in plain view is a source of tension, stress, and guilt.

Organizing paperwork piles can be rewarding because it is the fastest way to clear space and simplify your life. Most people agree and say paper is their biggest problem. But having the desire and actually conquering your paper pile are two different things.

If you are ready and motivated, you can put together paper systems that will keep your daily paperwork under control. If you have a consistent habit in one area (such as folding your towels, hanging your keys on the same hook, keeping an organized computer or CD collection), it is possible to transfer that skill to other areas, especially organizing paperwork.

Easier said than done? Not if you truly want to simplify your paperwork space. You must learn how to deal with daily papers until the space is working and simple.

Create a Plan

Did you know that fifteen pieces of mail arrive in the average household every day? Add to that mix flyers at your front door, paper from work, receipts from the grocery store, and papers from your child's school—and you have an overflowing counter full of paper.

When you see a step you can do, put down the book and go do it. After all, the goal of this book is to motivate and inspire you to take action to simplify your space.

Choose one counter by your telephone and monthly calendar to arrange as a personal organizing center for your daily paperwork. This is a mini-office to handle the day's mail, kids' school papers, and even bill paying if you wish. (You can view "before and after" pictures of kitchens with personal organizing centers on my Web site: www.organizingpro.com.)

SPACE-SAVING TIP #9

Simplify your life by organizing daily paperwork into file folders, three-ring binders, or computer files.

Simplify Your Daily Paperwork

Motivation:

- I want to get organized and keep up on paperwork.
- I don't want paper littering my house.
- I need a better paper system.

Supplies:

- Office supplies: paper clips, stapler, sticky notes, notepad
- Wastebasket and recycle bin
- File folders and labels (or label maker)

Time Estimate:

2 hours, depending on the backlog

Reward:

Only fifteen to twenty minutes a day to handle incoming mail and paperwork.

You simplify your life when you organize your daily incoming paperwork. That means a file to organize every paper, a place where action steps are written down, and supply drawer or tray nearby to complete an action are readily accessible without leaving the space.

Approach It by Sections

The mail can be the source of your paper pile problems, but that can be solved! Set up five file folders by your phone and monthly calendar where you open the mail. This is usually a two-foot counter space by your telephone.

Mail

Simplify your mail by sorting daily mail into the following five file folders:

File Folder #1—Calendar. Mark your calendar with the event and then file the paper in this folder until you need it. List the date in the upper right corner of the paper and keep these papers in time order, with the next event in the front for easy retrieval.

File Folder #2—To Do. List the to-do item on a master list on the counter or in your daily planner. Assign it to one of the three days you can most control: today, tomorrow, or the next day. Then file the single paper into the to-do folder. If a to-do item has more than one paper, create a new file folder for that project.

File Folder #3—To Decide. Place papers you might take action on in this file until you make that decision to move ahead. That includes things to order, do, or sign up for and will clear a lot of your paper pile off the kitchen counter.

File Folder #4—Information. Include seasonal sports schedules, neighborhood phone lists, polling place, and community information in this file to refer to in the future.

File Folder #5—My Interests. Corral personal papers like fitness center coupons, decorating ideas, or thank-you notes in this file to retrieve at a moment's notice.

Label additional files that are needed, such as a file for each person in the family. Place a paper in the front of each person's file to jot down things to talk about the next time he or she goes through the file. Hopefully that will be daily for the children or on the weekends for a spouse.

Bills

You need one place to file your bills until it is time to pay them. Organize a container with the soonest bill to pay in front, writing the date you need to send it where the stamp goes on the envelope. Consider getting a thirteen-slot accordion file to put the paid bills and receipts in once they are paid. File these records by the months of the year or by topic.

Magazines

A basket or coffee table is a typical place for new magazines. But the challenge is to follow a system of what to do with the previous ones. You can cut out articles you still want to read and toss the rest of the magazine. Or you can file the prior one in a magazine holder and only keep the issues that fit in your holder.

Evaluate if you are really reading the magazines. If you are three months or more behind in your reading, it's probably time to let the subscription drop the next time it comes up. Read the magazine at the library or online if it really interests you.

1. Create a Personal Organizing Center
2. Set Up Five File Folders
3. Organize Mail, Bills, Paperwork

Newspapers

Too many newspapers signals that you have too much to read, too little time to spend reading, or that you are trying to read too much.

Reduce your newspaper subscriptions to the ones you have time and interest in reading daily. Learn to read the headlines of the first page of each section, or go directly to the sections that appeal to you. Finish in the time you allocate for reading. Fifteen minutes a day or half an hour for a weekend paper is normal.

To make sure your paperwork stays in order, recycle your newspaper each day (or every week). And keep your newspaper in one spot, such as the family room table or kitchen counter.

Catalogs

There's one simple rule for catalogs: new one in, old one out. That's because the company will continue to send you updated catalogs. Look through it once and turn down the right-hand page corner of things you're interested in. Go back and pick one or two items you will most likely purchase. You can clip those, put them in your "To Decide" folder, and toss the catalog immediately. Otherwise, file catalogs alphabetically in magazine holders.

School Papers

Determine where your kids should put their backpacks after school and exactly where they should put any school papers. Place papers to return in backpacks each night before bed. Graded papers can be reviewed together daily or on the weekend, and the best one placed on the refrigerator.

On the weekend or on a school vacation day, spend fifteen minutes going through accumulated papers and put your child's favorites in a three-ring binder. Label tabs for each grade level so it becomes a "memory book." Display them on their birthday or holidays with relatives. Generally, four binders hold birth through high school papers, artwork, and childhood awards—and these are a great present for when they marry or move into their own apartment. It shows you are proud of them.

Work Papers

The best way to keep work-related papers from overtaking your home space is to work on them in one place (such as a desk or kitchen table) and put them away in your briefcase or laptop carrier. Then they will be sure to get back to work the next day.

If you work at home extensively, then you need to set up a home office. For more information on setting up and simplifying your home office, see chapter 10.

SPACE-SAVING TIP #10

A good guideline for magazines and catalogs is "New one in, old one out"—even if you have to read the old one on the spot.

Refrigerator

Only the top third of the refrigerator face should hold strategically placed papers: school papers of each child, family photos, a grocery list (with a pen), and items of significance to you. To maintain an uncluttered look in your kitchen, avoid using your refrigerator as a bulletin board.

Special photos can be placed in clear magnet holders on the refrigerator, and the rest either in a photo book or a photo box with the newest ones in front. Be sure to label the season and year on the back of each one.

Mark any appointments on your family calendar and file appointment cards in the "Calendar" file.

Lighten Up and Let Go

The best way to lighten up your daily paperwork is to look at the entire process of mail and paperwork for the day and ask, "Do I have the time to do all this? And do I want to?"

If the answer is no, then decide what you will spend time on:

KEEP	TOSS
Put bills into your bill-paying box.	Discard advertisements to purchase additional items.
File grocery coupons and coupons for your three favorite restaurants.	Toss grocery circulars and coupon fliers after looking them over.
Display one to three of your favorite magazines or catalogs.	Don't renew subscriptions for magazines you haven't had time to read lately.

SPACE-SAVING TIP #11

Organize children's school papers by using a color-coded folder for each child. The right pocket always contains papers coming home and the left pocket holds papers to go back to school. Check this daily to help your children succeed.

Daily Paperwork Checklist

____ 1. Do I know what papers pile up and create problems?

____ 2. Do I have file folders (or something similar) to deal with each day's mail?

____ 3. Is there a personal organizing center by my phone and monthly calendar to handle the day's papers?

____ 4. Do I have a bill-paying spot and a regular time to pay bills each month?

____ 5. Do I have a system to keep magazines and catalogs current?

____ 6. Are newspapers on a weekly recycling system?

____ 7. Do we have a place and system for schoolwork to go to and from school each day?

____ 8. Is there a regular place for work items and my computer case?

____ 9. Is my refrigerator door clutter free except for the top one-third of special items?

____ 10. Are my daily papers neatly filed and getting done?

Tips from "The Decorating Coach," Susan Wells

Even organizing systems can look attractive while they perform everyday tasks. Divider trays, paper clip holders, and storage bins are available in a number of finishes. Determine which storage devices you require and then purchase a style that blends with your decor.

Leather pieces lend an air of sophistication, mesh sets reflect a casual decor, Plexiglas adds a contemporary flair, and woven basket holders create a down-home country feel.

What style would you like your work area to convey? You'll enjoy using accessories that also make a fashion statement. It costs so little to capture your unique decorating style.

Manage It Simply

Today the kitchen counter mail pile and recycle bin are not the only tools to handle your mail. You can improve and manage your system by setting up file folders to keep track of your daily paperwork.

- One client spent a Saturday sorting, labeling, and filing her papers in her personal organizing center. She said, "My husband was so amazed that he cooked dinner just so I could keep working. After I went to bed, I ran downstairs five different times just to look at the clean space. We're thrilled."

- Another client and I set up a personal organizing center to handle the day's papers, but she still had a backlog, which she planned to sort a little each day. Finally after months of not getting anywhere, she sat down and spent one entire day getting it all sorted, filed, and tossed. "It's done!" she exclaimed with pride. "And I couldn't feel better, even though it took me twelve hours! Now I can keep up because I decided what's really important on a daily basis."

- Jacob was annoyed with his wife insisting that he go through the mail and children's papers every night. After a few days of consideration, they came up with a plan. Linda would sort the mail each day, but because of his paper-intensive job as an administrator, he would go through all the home paperwork on the weekend. He knew it would take two hours, but it worked because they both kept up their part. And Linda alerted her husband to any paperwork that needed attention each day.

Review: The CALM Paperwork Approach

Create a Plan
○ Set up a personal organizing center for mail.
○ Get a desk tray divider and arrange your five files.
○ Plan to set up systems to handle papers sitting in piles.

Approach It by Sections
○ Put papers in file folders or a labeled three-ring binder.
○ Decide where magazines and catalogs will go.
○ Keep bills in a designated holder and pay them on time.

Lighten Up and Let Go
○ Fill and empty the recycle bin and shredder often.
○ Unsubscribe from magazines and catalogs that clutter your life.
○ Organize and file necessary papers well.

Manage It Simply
Daily—Spend twenty minutes a day or two hours per week sorting your mail.
Weekly—Empty the recycle bin.
Monthly—Go through your files and toss expired coupons, event fliers, etc.

Organizing your daily paperwork can significantly lower your stress, save you money, and simplify your space. Learn to be decisive and readily toss paper. Never give up on your goals to keep a clean paper setup that looks nice and works well.

Setting up the tools of a daily paperwork system is only half the story;
setting up regular routines and habits is the other half. Any organizational system,
by the way, consists of two components which make this simple equation:
A system = tools + habits.

—SUSAN SILVER

Simplify Your Personal Space

Once you've covered the visible spaces of your house, it's time to give your personal space the time and attention it needs. In the midst of your busy life, you may be overlooking these three busy spaces: bedrooms, the closets, and the bathroom. The goal is to simplify these spaces so everyone can get an easy start in the morning and come home to order later in the day.

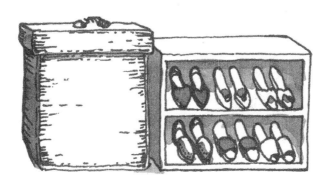

5

Simplify Your Bedroom

The bedroom is a sanctuary, the place where you retreat after
a long, hard day. Of all the rooms in your home, this one
should be the most free of distractions.

—MERYL STARR

The most restful room in your home is the one we often give the least attention—
the bedroom. This is the place from which we launch our day and to which we
retreat at night.

Now why would simplifying this room be so hard to do? As someone once said, if
all there was to organizing a bedroom is making the bed, it would be the easiest room
in the house to keep clean. Actually, once you make the bed the room *is* 50 to 70 percent clean, so that is an excellent way to start every day!

My client Mary Ann's bedroom looked like she had just hosted a teenage sleepover.
Another client couple had the opposite problem—nothing but a bed frame and an old
bedspread graced the room. Is there a balance between form and function for your
bedroom? Or is it like Mary Ann said: "It's my room, so who cares?"

You should care. Waking up to a clean, organized room has a positive effect on your
outlook. It is the one place to find comfort before facing the world for the day. Don't let
your bedroom decline just because it's not a "company showpiece." It's your most personal
space, so let's make it one of your favorite spaces and the foundation of an orderly life.

Create a Plan

A fair number of people dive right into organizing the bedroom and end up with stacks of items on the floor they intend to deliver, donate, or discard. But does that approach work? As a general rule, no. You want a plan that will leave the bedroom clear of clutter. You can do it with only a one-time cleanup plus a small step each day so you can finish the room in no time at all.

Our plan for simplifying your bedroom has three steps. We will deal with the largest to the smallest visible areas. Our goal is a peaceful and pleasant room to sleep well and relax in.

The spaces you can easily assess include:

- Large surfaces: bed and floor
- Flat surfaces: dresser tops, nightstands, under the bed
- Interior surfaces: drawers, shelves, boxes

Simplify Your Bedroom

Motivation:
- I'd like to clear the clutter out of my bedroom.
- I want my bedroom to be a restful haven.
- My bedroom is the last thing I decorated, and I need to finish.

Supplies:
- Wastebasket and recycle bin for items to be discarded
- Three boxes for things to put away, donate, and sell
- Pen and notepad

Time Estimate:
2–3 hours

Reward:
A peaceful room to wake up in each morning and return to each night.

If you are like many people who are often in a rush, your bedroom is the place you tend to lay things down, instead of putting them away. Or it's the place to hide Christmas presents, put the sewing machine, or stash a desk for some quiet workspace.

Take a moment to stand at the doorway to your bedroom and ask the following questions:

1. What needs the most attention to simplify this bedroom? The bed, the floor clutter, flat surfaces?
2. Is the room visually clean but the drawers and shelves full of clutter you'd like to let go of?
3. Is it a pretty room, or does it need a facelift with new paint and bedspread?

Now, let's begin to work our plan with your answers in mind.

Approach It by Sections

The goal of simplifying your bedroom is having a restful, enjoyable space at the beginning and end of the day. You can do these short steps in ten minutes a day until you are finished, or you could set aside a day and put it together.

Start with the large and most visible surfaces, such as the bed and floor.

Bed

Begin by washing the bedding and making the bed. While you are at it, vacuum the mattress and turn it over (if it does so). Now that the bed is made, half or more of your room is truly clean. Nothing feels better than a freshly made bed.

If your bedspread looks worn or you need new pillow shams or a headboard, you may want to start looking for new bedding. Add a matching headboard or pictures over the headboard to make an attractive focal point.

Floor

The next largest surface in your bedroom is the floor, so be sure to vacuum the floor often, especially before you begin working on the drawers and shelves. Sort through any items that may be in piles around your bedroom until you can see a clean floor.

Do you need new carpet or area rug? If you can work it into your budget, now would be a good time to treat yourself to a floor covering that makes your toes happy to be barefoot each night.

Piles

Piles on the floor in the bedroom usually shrink the size of the room. So empty the contents of cardboard boxes, laundry baskets, and bags by dealing with each pile. Always keep this in mind: *one pile is the beginning of losing control of a neat room.*

SPACE-SAVING TIP #12

Stand at the doorway to your bedroom and look for clean, uncluttered dresser tops, floor, and neatly made bed to keep your bedroom restful.

Clothes

Cut your bedroom cleanup time in half by putting your clothes immediately back on hangers, folded in the drawer, or in the clothes hamper. Nothing makes a bedroom look messy faster than clothes draped across a chair or piled on the floor.

The same goes for clean laundry. Put clean clothes away before the next meal so you never walk in to see clothes sitting out.

Dresser and Nightstands

Now that the bed is made and the floor is clear, look at the flat surfaces in your bedroom to purge the clutter and put away "homeless" items.

How many flat surfaces do you have in the bedroom: a dresser and a nightstand or more? Count them now. This is the number you want to clear and organize this week. These furniture pieces can make your bedroom restful or stressful.

Begin by emptying and dusting each dresser top one at a time, putting useful and attractive objects in the back third of each space. This allows a clear line of sight as your eye sweeps over the room and it looks organized and peaceful.

The problems occur when books stack up, clothes don't get put away, magazines are temporarily set down, and watches and coins clutter the dresser top. Be careful! Keep your dresser surfaces clean by containerizing items in the top drawers and designating places for the "homeless" items cluttering up the visual space in the room.

1. Make Your Bed Daily
2. Clear Flat Surfaces
3. Organize Drawers and Cabinets

SPACE-SAVING TIP #13

Choose several types of lighting for your bedroom to create an inviting ambience—a bedside reading light, soft dresser lighting, and candles to beckon you home at night.

Nightstands

Keep current reading material, decorative items, and a reading lamp on your nightstand. The challenge is to stick with one or two books until they are finished and keep the surface intentionally organized with only your clock, music, and current magazine or book. Keep just what you will use, and designate places elsewhere for the excess items.

Keep your nightstand from becoming a leaning tower with stacks of books you have started but haven't finished. Limit your reading to two books at a time, and store the rest on bookshelves. Place magazines neatly in a magazine holder or basket, and be sure to recycle previous issues.

Under the Bed

The space under your bed is perfect for under-the-bed boxes to store a holiday wrapping center or out-of-season clothes. If you have drawers under your bed, you can store current reading materials out of sight too.

Dresser Drawers

Before you open each dresser drawer, think about what category of items you would *like* to be inside. Then open the drawer, take everything out, and sort as you go into three piles: "Keep" items on the far right in front of you, "maybe keep" items in the middle behind the drawer, and "get rid of" items to your left. Have two receptacles on your left: a trash bag and a donation bag.

Start from the top drawer of a dresser and work downward. Put in gift boxes as dividers or buy containers that fit the drawer to keep items from sliding into a heap.

Once you put in your dividers, put items you use most often in the front, things used less often in the middle, and storage items in the back. Leave 20 percent of the visible space empty for a spacious feeling and room for new things inside the drawer.

Then deliver the trash bag and donation bag. Keep the drawer neat and put something pretty in it to make you smile when you open it. You'll be more likely to keep it organized.

SPACE-SAVING TIP #14

Retire to bed a few minutes early to enjoy a magazine or novel. You can get through an amazing number of books by reading one chapter each night.

Shelves

Sort one shelf at a time from the top shelving down. Begin by removing everything and wiping off the shelf. Now sort the items on your bed or clean floor: "keep" items to the right, "maybe keep" items in the middle, and "get rid of" items on the left into a trash bag or donation bag.

Put back items by categories: books together, labeled magazine holders on shelving, decorative items displayed. Leave space between items and add a plant, figurine, or clock to blend "hardscape" items with "softscape" items to make an interesting landscape on your shelving in the bedroom.

Armoire

A closed armoire or chest can become a clutter space unless you sort it regularly. Again, start from the top down and go through shelf by shelf and drawer by drawer. Once you return your armoire to its organized state, you can breeze through getting ready each morning.

If your armoire houses your TV, DVDs, and CDs, cull through your media collection so your bedroom armoire contains only the top ten tunes and movies you currently enjoy. Make sure your TV is positioned so that it is easy to see, and make your sound system part of the restful atmosphere of your bedroom.

A chest at the foot of the bed is a great place to store blankets and heirlooms. If you have one, empty it out and put back only what you use and foresee as heirlooms to pass on to your family. Don't keep anything you don't like or anything that is stained. Fix it up or get rid of it.

Lighten Up and Let Go

Let the bedroom be the one personal space you stay on top of for order and peace—your personal haven of rest each day. Move it from stressful to restful by clearing the surfaces, ordering the drawers, and letting go of excess clutter.

A good cleaning in the fall and spring when you clean your clothes closet will keep this room in order. Maintain that order by developing a lifelong habit of making your bed each day. It only takes a minute and a half to make the bed for sixteen hours of order in this room!

Bedroom Checklist

____ 1. Is the bed made and easy to make each day?

____ 2. Is the floor clear of piles and clothes?

____ 3. Are the dresser tops clear on the front two-thirds and attractively arranged in the back?

____ 4. Are under-the-bed boxes storing useful items in usable containers?

____ 5. Are the dresser drawers organized, and do the drawers open easily?

_____ 6. Are the shelves organized and attractive?

_____ 7. Is the armoire or chest neatly housing items that are important to me now?

_____ 8. Is the TV easy to see and the sound system part of the restful atmosphere?

_____ 9. Are there any piles that need to be put away?

_____ 10. Is the bedroom attractive, restful, and clutter free?

Tips from "The Decorating Coach," Susan Wells

Add punch with a pillow: that's the secret weapon that designers use to add the "wow factor" to rooms. Large sizes are in, and pillows are the least expensive way to redecorate a room. Pillows can introduce a new accent color without changing the main elements. Repeat the same fabric in other areas like a drapery tieback or table runner.

Incorporate tassels or buttons onto your existing pillows to transform them from ho-hum to show-stopping. Make a pillow or ask a friend to help. Just one yard of top-of-the-line fabric creates a couple of pillows that will become the focal point of your room. Watch for sales or shop at discount outlets to pick up eye-catching designs.

Manage It Simply

Clutter can steal the restfulness out of what should be the most peaceful room of your home. Keep your bedroom clean with a quick two-minute pickup each morning and evening. When the seasons change for spring and fall, organize a dresser drawer a day from top to bottom to change over to the next season's clothes.

- Patty was a well-organized lady who had a "center" for each of her interests and projects. The problem was her sewing projects, office desk, and ironing basket turned her bedroom from a retreat into a barricade to keep the children out. And her husband didn't feel welcome either.

We reclaimed Patty's bedroom by moving the sewing machine to the closet, the ironing board to the laundry room, and placing a freestanding divider around the desk. Her bedroom started to feel like a home instead of a mini apartment.

- Joan, a busy homeschooling mom with six children, collected all the single socks in large laundry baskets by the side of her bed. What had become a project sitting in her bedroom became a permanent nightstand of stacked baskets—until we spread them on the bed and paired the matching socks. We found one large basket full of white socks and one equally large basket for colored socks. She had intended to sort them, but never seemed to have time.

  After half an hour of matching socks, she let the unmatched single socks (and two laundry baskets) go. Her bedroom improved dramatically, and so did romance when all the undone projects were banned from the bedroom!

- George was a technology fan and had been since the 1970s. The problem was that his equipment was also from the '70s: large speakers, an old VCR, two partially working radios, and a cassette player with a portable CD player rigged up to boot. Rather than buy new equipment, George continued to add to his collection and focused on "function" without much thought to "form."

  After much discussion, he finally compromised with his wife by buying a high-end new system for Christmas. The problem was still parting with the old equipment. But since electronics sell well at garage sales, he eventually let his vintage equipment go for some cash.

Review: The CALM Bedroom Approach

Create a Plan
○ Large surfaces first
○ Flat surfaces second
○ Interior spaces third

Approach It by Sections
○ Clothes drawers
○ Jewelry drawers
○ Activity areas of reading, exercise, crafts

Lighten Up and Let Go
○ Charity donations: extra bedding, knickknacks, or unwanted jewelry
○ Clothes: Put in the closet, hamper, or donate
○ Papers, CDs, DVDs: move to the office or family room

Manage It Simply
Daily—Every morning, make your bed and put away out-of-place items on top of dressers and on the floor in a two-minute sweep.
Weekly—Clean, dust, vacuum, and straighten the bedroom to keep it attractive and inviting.
Monthly—Review the contents of your drawers and shelves and keep giving away excess until these spaces are easy to maintain.

   Your bedroom should be the most restful place in your home. I encourage you to give it the attention it needs to best serve as the "bookends" of your day. If you keep working on your bedroom one step at a time, you will soon have an organized and pleasant space to spend time each day.

Bedrooms are to the home what the easy chair is to the end of a hard day.
—MAXINE ORDESKY

6

Simplify Your
Bedroom Closet

Perhaps in no other area are we more tempted to keep
unused things than with clothes. Listen, let's quit dreaming. Give it
to the Salvation Army. Let them find the perfect person.

—SANDRA FELTON

M a'am, I need to know how much hanging space you need before I can build your new closets," the project manager told my client.

Lindsay's family was living with three-foot-square closets in a turn-of-the-century historic home. She was desperate to find out how to maximize her closet space! But she didn't know how to answer the project manager's question.

"How would I know how much hanging space I need?" she asked.

"Oh, that's simple. Just count the hangers you have, allow an inch and a half per hanger, and then tell me how many feet of rod hanging space you need," he replied.

My client smiled and flicked her hand. "Of course I thought he was kidding, since I had no time to do that! But my engineer husband patiently counted the hangers and came back with the news."

"'Honey, we've got a big problem,'" he said. "'I don't know how to tell you this, but we need a quarter mile of hanging space!'"

When Lindsay told me this story, we both laughed as we realized how vast that closet would be. How had so much accumulated when she wasn't looking? Or had she reached the limit of what she could realistically live with and take care of?

I suspect that there is a bit of Lindsay in each of us—too many clothes, belts, or handbags, matched by too much jewelry and sportswear that is taking up needed space in our closets. Today is the day to simplify your bedroom closet! If you had to count every single item, how many items would you have to sort through to get dressed each day? Likely too many. Let's go through your closet and find out.

Create a Plan

The goal for simplifying closet space is to organize and downscale so three things happen: getting dressed each morning is an easy part of your day, you walk out wearing a tasteful outfit, and you come back to an organized closet at the end of the day.

In this chapter, I will show you not only how to organize your closet but how to simplify it so you can get dressed easily. As you sort through the things in your closet, ask two key questions over each article of clothing: "Do I like this? Am I wearing it now (or in the near future)?" If the answer is no to either one, then out it goes!

I like one retailer's motto: "A closet full of clothes you can wear." We usually have the first part—a full closet—but it's not full of things we can wear. There's a lot more in there that we need to weed out regularly, usually in the fall and spring, to pass on the excess we've accumulated.

Here's the order for our sorting:

1. Everything hanging
2. Everything on the floor
3. Everything on the shelves
4. Everything in drawers

If you need help making decisions, ask a friend who is decisive and dresses similarly and a bit better than you. The more organized your closet is the less time it should take. The more disorganized it is, the happier you will be when you see the finished result.

Simplify Your Bedroom Closet

Motivation:

- I can't find things I want in my closet.
- I have nothing to wear.
- I want to save time getting ready in the morning.

Supplies:

- Three boxes for items to give away, dry clean, and fix
- Labels or label maker
- Matching hangers (all one style)

Time Estimate:

4–8 hours per closet

Reward:

An organized closet of ready-to-wear outfits

The problem with the closet often is too much stuff and disorganized space which makes Pareto's "20–80 Rule" true. Because we have too many clothes, we are often reaching for the favorite 20 percent of our clothes and searching through the not-so-favorite 80 percent that is taking up valuable space. Let's move the 80 percent unused items out and enjoy the organized space as well as benefiting other people.

Approach It by Sections

Start organizing your closet by making your bed, so you have a flat surface to do any necessary sorting. Designate a bag or box for "giveaway" clothes, plus two others for "fix" and "dry clean."

Hanging Clothes

Start at one end of the closet rod and sort the hanging clothes. Pull out each item and ask yourself these two questions: "Do I like this? Do I wear it now?" If the answer is no, place the item in your "giveaway" box. If the answer is yes, then rehang the clothes by categories, such as long-sleeved tops, short-sleeved tops, slacks, and jackets. Step up your organization by arranging each section from dark colors to light colors, like a rainbow. Often you will find too many of the same color or style, so keep the best and let go of the rest.

Now finish the hanging items by using matching hangers and placing the front of the clothing items toward you. Hangers should hang one and a half inches apart. You should be able to see the front easily when you are looking for something to wear. Place your most used items closest to you.

If you have nice clothes but feel like you have nothing to wear, put together an outfit you like, including the jewelry, shoes, and purse. Take a picture and post it in your closet. Then on those days when you can't think of anything to wear, you can go to your tried-and-true photos to find a presentable (and sensational) outfit.

Store items elsewhere that you might still wear—another size, another season, or old favorites. This storage under the bed or in another closet should be less than a third of your current wardrobe, or you may be storing postponed decisions. Decide now to let go!

SPACE-SAVING TIP #15

Pull out all your empty hangers and develop the habit of putting them at one end of the closet. Space saved? Three inches for every dozen empty hangers.

Closet Floor

Organize the closet floor by pulling everything out and organizing your shoes. This is where dust and clutter most accumulate, so I suggest you clean and vacuum the floor before going through your shoes.

Line up your shoes from dressy to casual and dark to light. Do you have room for all of them? If not, weed out the least worn or most scuffed-up shoes. Now you have new space! Make a note to get a shoe storage system that holds what you own.

- Get matching boxes for other storage items on your closet floor and label them for a clean and tidy look.
- Toss any plastic bags, as they tend to look messy and create floor clutter.

- Don't forget to include a clothes hamper in your closet or nearby.
- Polish and clean your shoes. Box out-of-season shoes on your shelves with a label on the front. When you rotate them seasonally, turn the box around and put a second label on the backside of the box for a different season.

Realtors say you can increase buyer appeal by keeping the floor of your closet relatively empty and clean. That's a good everyday practice too.

SPACE-SAVING TIP #16

A variation on hanging clothes in blouse-slacks-jacket categories is to hang five of your favorite everyday outfits together, so it's easy to "grab and go."

1. Sort Hanging Clothes
2. Organize the Floor Items
3. Simplify the Shelves

Mirror

A full-length mirror in or near your closet is your best tool for dressing nicely. Hang one on your closet door or prop one up in your bedroom. Check your appearance from head to toe to look your best for the day.

Trust your instincts to improve your clothes, shoes, and jewelry. And if it's a bad hair day, just smile extra big!

Shelves

Take everything off your closet shelves and put back only what you like and use. Shelves often contain sweaters, purses, hats, shoeboxes, bags, and T-shirts that were once daily regulars in your life. But over time these belongings turn into "stationary" clutter that doesn't know when to leave.

Now is the time to make those hard decisions and let some things go. Ask yourself, "Is this item part of my past or my future?" If it's sentimental, take a picture and let it go! This is your everyday closet. Save the memory in a picture, not on your shelf.

- Refold sweaters so the smooth, rounded edge I call "the decorative edge" is facing you. This provides a neat, clean look like fine retailers and makes each sweater easy to slide out.
- Hook shelf dividers on a shelf to keep one stack of clothes from falling over. Or space shoeboxes between stacks of clothes and purses to hold items in place.
- Use clear boxes to see what is neatly placed inside, or label closed boxes so you don't have to see the contents daily but you still know what's inside.

SPACE-SAVING TIP #17

Invite a friend who dresses the way you like, but a bit better, to sort your closet with you. She and the mirror will give you the courage to let go of mismatched items and recycle the rest into your favorite style.

Closet Drawers

Sort your closet or dresser drawers one at a time and use them efficiently for storing clothes and dressing items. Sort items by the size of the items, and then place them in that size drawer. For instance, keep jewelry in jewelry trays in the narrowest drawers. Place socks and scarves in other narrow drawers. Stack T-shirts and sweaters neatly folded in deeper drawers. To see what is at the bottom of a deep drawer, stair-step the T-shirts or sweaters with one inch of the item under it showing so you can see all the items easily.

- Store underwear in one drawer with dividers to keep them from sliding around. Have enough for two weeks.
- Roll slippery nightgowns and lingerie so each rounded edge faces you and is easy to lift out. Use a box divider to keep it from piling up in a heap.
- Hang everything you can and fold less wrinkly items (sweaters, T-shirts, and sportswear) in drawers.

Jewelry Drawers

Put earrings in a hanging holder or small dividers like a plastic craft box or colored egg holder. Get a fabric tray or standing necklace holder to keep necklaces untangled. Keep only jewelry that you currently use. Store your treasures and give away the rest. Organizing jewelry will save you lots of dressing time and make a good outfit great!

SPACE-SAVING TIP #18

You can save twenty-five loads of laundry a year by getting enough underwear for two weeks and washing it every other week.

Lighten Up and Let Go

We are trained to recycle lots of things. My plea is for you to actively rotate unused items out of your closet and into the hands of those who can use it.

After taking a trip to Haiti, I have personally been challenged to give away closet clutter. My feeling is you sometimes overlook your garage, knickknack, or book clutter, but people *need* your excess clothes. Recycle those unworn clothes today.

There are needy people in and around your city as well as around the world. So don't be guilty of hoarding unused items in closets and drawers. Give these items away, and people will be so happy to receive your excess treasures.

Bedroom Closet Checklist

____ 1. Are clothes hung by sections and outfits I like to wear?

____ 2. Do all my hangers match?

____ 3. Is my closet floor relatively empty and clutter free?

____ 4. Are my shoes organized and ready to wear at a moment's notice?

____ 5. Is there a full-length mirror nearby I use daily?

____ 6. Is the smooth "decorative edge" facing forward on all folded items?

____ 7. Does each drawer have clothes and accessories organized by category?

____ 8. Is my jewelry stored neatly in dividers and ready for me to dress quickly?

____ 9. Do I regularly give clothes away to benefit others?

____ 10. Is it easy to get dressed each day?

Tips from "The Decorating Coach," Susan Wells

Say farewell to boring closets with a few decorative accents. Hooks that have been embellished with extra detail are versatile yet charming. Pewter finishes add a crisp contrast to walls painted in cool shades; bronze hooks will stand out against warm colors.

Put your shoeboxes to imaginative use by covering them in a series of mix-and-match textures. Lightly apply spray-on glue to the sides, attach fabric that has been cut to size, and then repeat for the covers. Fill with shoes and accessories, then stack and store your beautiful boxes.

For a finishing touch, indulge yourself in pretty hangers. A series of rich woods will lend an air of sophistication and continuity along the rod.

Manage It Simply

Keep your closet and clothes in working order with a simple schedule. A penciled-in index card can be fine-tuned until you find a schedule that works for you. For example, a weekly clothes-maintenance schedule might look something like this:

SUNDAY	MONDAY	TUESDAY	WEDNESDAY	THURSDAY	FRIDAY	SATURDAY
	Wash whites	Drop off dry cleaning	Wash darks	Pick up dry cleaning	Wash shirts and iron	Free or catch-up day

A weekly routine will keep your clothes ready to wear anytime you need them. Every clothing item needs a home. A "stuffed" closet is a red flag that it's time to sort and donate the excess.

- Kathryn's girlfriends offered to come over one day and organize her closet with her. "Keep or go?" was the constant question to her as they went through one item at a time.

    When they were finished, one friend said, "I'm taking these giveaway clothes bags home for a week. You can call me if you need something, and I will retrieve it." Four days later Kathryn called when she needed a blouse for a suit. The friend returned the blouse—and that was the only item she retrieved.

    Kathryn's response? Gratitude that her friends helped her do what she couldn't do on her own. And she was relieved to dress better as well.

- After my seminar, Mary Ann went home and gave away all the shoes in her closet that were painful to wear or no longer fit—twenty-two pairs of shoes went to a charity! The charity was quite happy, and Mary Ann was too, once she replaced them with shoes that were comfortable.

- Kim said when she gives away an outfit, she gives the jewelry with it too. "Why not?' she said. "I picked the most sensational pieces when I bought the outfit, so now someone else can also save the time shopping and look great right away."

Review: The CALM Bedroom Closet Approach

Create a Plan
○ Hanging items first
○ Floor second
○ Shelves and drawers third

Approach It by Sections
○ Set out a donations box to fill.
○ Replace mismatched hangers with matching ones to inspire order.
○ Use matching containers and label shoeboxes.

Lighten Up and Let Go
○ Donate extra clothes, shoes, and jewelry to a charity or give them to someone you know.
○ Drop off items to be dry-cleaned or tailored.
○ Take pictures of clothes you pass on if you feel the need to keep the memory.

Manage It Simply
Daily—Straighten up before you leave each morning, and put your clothes on hangers and put away your shoes each evening.
Weekly—Keep filling your donation box with items you don't use.
Seasonally—Go through your clothes, shoes, and jewelry and get rid of those you no longer use or need.

Think of your closet as your most personal (and pleasant) space. Make a clean bedroom, an organized closet, and a tidy bathroom part of your routine to start and end your day right. You'll have a sense of serenity and well-being to face whatever happens each day.

Whenever clients describe certain items as Good Stuff, I point out that just because stuff is good doesn't mean it's good for them.

—HARRIET SCHECHTER

7

Simplify Your Bathroom

The idea is to get unwanted stuff out of your space as quickly
as possible. Successful purging is all about having the
undesirable objects out of sight, out of mind, and fast!

—CHRISTOPHER LOWELL

Someone once counted all the things a man and a woman hold in their bathroom.
It was estimated that a man has 11 items to a woman's 367, most of which a man
cannot identify! Based on those statistics, I bet you can guess who should take
charge of clearing and simplifying this room of your home.

Today, you will start simplifying your bathroom by sorting through the contents. If you
have more than one bathroom, sort only one bathroom at a time. The more often you do
this, the less time it will take . . . and the smoother your mornings and evenings will go.

Create a Plan

You might think a bathroom would be the easiest room to organize because it's the
smallest, right? Wrong. Its contents move quickly from a prized new skin-care regime
to outdated clutter sitting on the counter. The toothbrush holder holds toothbrushes
that should have been replaced long ago. And who knows exactly what is in the back
corner of the under-the-sink cabinet!

It's time to get this small space into shipshape order. We can do this easily by working in sections. Here's the order for our sorting:

1. Countertops
2. Shelves and drawers
3. Cabinet under the sink
4. Linen closet

The problem to overcome in a bathroom is how to make the best use of the space you have. You need to create room for towels, toiletries (anything in bottles, tubes, or jars), and appliances such as your hair dryer and curling iron.

Simplify Your Bathroom

Motivation:
- Company's coming!
- It's time for a good bathroom cleanup.
- I'm ready to sort through everything.

Supplies:
- Wastebasket and recycle bin for items to be discarded
- Donations box for items to be given away
- Labels and marker (or label maker)

Time Estimate:
2 hours

Reward:
A beautiful bathroom to use every morning and evening.

Approach It by Sections

The good news about simplifying your bathroom space is that your bathroom is smaller than the other rooms in your home. And at the end of the sorting time, you can treat yourself to a reward by getting new towels, adding drawer dividers, or updating your containers. Plan your reward as you work.

Countertops

First, clear off the counter around your sink. Your counter space may be three inches or three feet, but this area must be organized and clutter free to create a spacious feeling.

Put back only the items you like and currently use. Then ask yourself these questions:

- Do the toothbrushes and toothpaste have a home that is easy to reach and attractive? They can go in a toothbrush holder, the medicine cabinet, or drawer.
- Does the bar of soap or soap pump work for you, or do you want another kind?
- Are the towels getting hung up? If not, would another towel bar or hooks make it easier for hanging?

Become a problem solver as you look at each item you return to your counter area. Stand at the doorway and view your counter surfaces. Are the front two-thirds of your counters clean and empty while the back one-third contains useful and attractive items?

SPACE-SAVING TIP #19

Less is more in a bathroom. Use up sample bottles, tubes, and creams to keep clutter down to the essentials you like and use.

Be ruthless as you simplify your counter space, knowing that the fewer items you have on your counters, the easier your counters will be to clean. Place bottles (such as makeup and lotions) on a tray so you can lift the tray when you clean instead of lifting each item.

A basket works wonders for neatly holding items like hand towels and guest lotions. Try to minimize the cords by placing your hair dryer and curling iron in a corner or putting them away in a drawer or cabinet after each use.

If the room looks too sterile, add something decorative like silk flowers or a candle. If it still has too much "cute" clutter, put some away and rotate these items for a new look each season. (But then you have complicated your life by having to do that regularly. Simplify instead!)

Shelves and Drawers

Next, organize your bathroom shelves and drawers one at a time. Begin with the worst one so you can see progress immediately. Or start top down in the medicine cabinet. Shelves are easy to sort if you stick to one at a time.

Whether sorting a shelf or a drawer, follow this three-step process:

1. Empty everything from one shelf onto the counter.
2. Wipe off the shelf or clean out the drawer.
3. Put back by category only what is currently useful.

For example, line up medications and skin-care products from left to right in the order you use them. Put toothbrushes, floss, and mouthwash on another shelf. Hairbrushes, combs, and barrettes deserve their own shelf so you won't end up with hair in your toothbrush!

As you empty a drawer or shelf, group items into three distinct locations: Place "keep" items to your right on the counter, "maybe keep" items in the middle, and "get rid of" items into a trash bag or donation box on the left.

SPACE-SAVING TIP #20

Organize a large cabinet with containers, baskets, or rollout shelving to keep items easy to retrieve and use.

As you sort your drawers, you can maintain order longer between cleanings by placing drawer dividers inside. That way, every item has a home and you can easily spot something out of place.

Before you buy dividers, choose the most accessible drawers (closest to waist height and easy reach) for the most often used items. Don't put the hairbrush you use every day too low while the cotton swabs you use once a month are in a prime location. Organize items based on frequency of use.

Spend fifteen minutes per drawer or shelf, and you will quickly be finished. Either stop at that point and deliver excess items to your donation boxes or keep going into the cabinets.

1. Clear the Countertops
2. Organize the Drawers
3. Simplify the Cabinets

Cabinets

Next, sort the cabinet under the bathroom sink and any other cabinets in your bathroom. The cabinet under the sink should be emptied and sorted often (as unpleasant as it may seem) because this is considered the "garage of the bathroom," where things you may not use anymore are put temporarily. As you probably already realize, temporary items become permanent clutter when you neglect regularly sorting an active space.

Empty everything out of the cabinet and group items into one of three areas: "keep" items to your right on the counter, "maybe keep" items in the middle and "get rid of" items on the left into a trash bag or donation box.

Then follow this simple process:

1. Wash out the cabinet shelves.
2. Plan containers or portable shelves to expand the space.
3. Return "keep" items into their new containers and label them.

SPACE-SAVING TIP #21

Find space you never thought you had in your linen closet by storing bed-sheets and towels in your bedroom closet and bathroom.

Under a sink, keep the first three to four inches empty to create the impression of an organized cabinet. Rethink how you store things under the sink and see if you can put towels closer to the shower and toilet paper in a container next to the toilet. A small bathroom stores it under the sink cabinet while a medium or larger bathroom can house it elsewhere. Adjust your storage needs to the space you have.

For a quick cleanup each week, keep cleaning supplies to dry the surfaces under the sink. A towel bar or hook inside the cabinet door can hold a towel so you can wipe off daily water spots too.

Linen Closet

Since the bathroom is often small, supplies can extend into a linen closet nearby. The linen closet can hold bath towels and bed linens, or you could reclaim the space.

Count the shelves in your linen closet and decide which ones are working for you. Empty the most used shelf, wipe it off, and replace with useful items.

Regain storage space in the linen closet by:

- Putting sheets in each bedroom closet shelf where they are used.
- Storing towels on shelves above the toilet or storing under the sink.
- Giving away mismatched towels, rags, and blankets you never use, or relegating them to the garage as rags.

Now use the linen closet as a hall closet and store things you've never had room for—bulk purchases of items, craft or photo supplies, vacuum cleaner, suitcases, sleeping bags, or a memory for each child.

The linen closet has great potential to house your new projects once you ruthlessly go through and get rid of items that are no longer a part of your life. Take them to charity and create new purposes for the space.

For example, my client Kathy loved making Creative Memory scrapbooks, but the photos and products were in clear plastic boxes cluttering the floor in her home office. She solved the problem by emptying her linen closet and reorganizing her Creative Memories box containers to fit. Now her home office is clean, the clutter in the linen closet is gone, and her scrapbooking supplies are readily available whenever she needs them.

Lighten Up and Let Go

Bathrooms are notorious for collecting unused shampoos, soaps, hair, and makeup products. Remember, less is more in a bathroom. Be sure to discard old items when you replace them with a newer or better product. Don't let unused toiletries create long-term clutter problems in the shower, bathtub, or medicine cabinet.

Medications should be sorted regularly to be sure they haven't passed their expiration dates. If they have, flush them down the toilet or take them back to your pharmacist for disposal. When you need to renew a prescription, call immediately so you have a day or two to pick it up.

Bathroom Checklist

_____ 1. Are countertops clear except for the back one-third of useful items?

_____ 2. Are cabinet shelves uncluttered and streamlined?

_____ 3. Do the drawers have dividers, and does everything have a place?

_____ 4. Are cleaning supplies and other items in containers and easy to use?

_____ 5. Do I have minimum cleaning supplies for maximum cleanup?

_____ 6. Are linen closet shelves holding useful items and decorative edges facing forward?

_____ 7. Are excess towels and sheets gone?

_____ 8. Are all medications current and useful?

_____ 9. Are old items tossed when replaced with new ones?

_____ 10. Is the bathroom functional and inviting?

Tips from "The Decorating Coach," Susan Wells

For amazing impact, mount a 24" x 30" picture on a blank wall. A small print by itself will float aimlessly. Give it profile by combining with a grouping of complementary hangings.

The softness and shape of towels will offset the coldness of the tub, tile, and sink. Indulge in a set of fluffy new ones. Layer them, folds to the front, over the toilet tank or on a shelf. Install an extra towel bar and wrap guest towels with raffia or ribbon.

For that "spa effect," display a collection of soaps, creams, and oils in an attractive bowl or basket. At least one color should flow through all these elements.

Manage It Simply

Here are some tips to help you keep your newly organized bathroom in great shape:

- Anything you purchase as a liquid, such as makeup, nail polish, or shampoo, is yours. You can't give it away to a charity or anyone else. So make sure all those toiletries you spend good money on are your favorites and ones you love to use.

- Dentists recommend that you purchase a new toothbrush every six months. To remember to do this, give yourself a new toothbrush as a birthday gift and six months later on your half birthday. Also, replace your toothbrush anytime you've had a virus, such as strep throat, to avoid recontamination.

- There are more bathroom cleaners available than people can try. Line up all your cleaning supplies for the bathroom and put them in priority order of what you use most. Then streamline the group by testing to see which ones can accomplish cleaning several surfaces at once. Can your countertop and sink cleaner also be used to wipe down fixtures? Which one cleaner works for your shower walls or toilet bowl? It's best to keep a window cleaner and dry towel in each bathroom in case you have unexpected company and need to do a quick cleanup. If you keep the bathroom counter and floor clean, your guests will say, "My, your house is so clean!" And it actually is!

Review: The CALM Bathroom Approach

Create a Plan
○ Countertops first
○ Cabinets and drawers second
○ Linen closet third

Approach It by Sections
○ Get your supplies for sorting: trash, donate, or put away.
○ Spend only fifteen minutes per drawer or shelf.
○ Speed sort by deciding aloud about each item, "Keep or go?"

Lighten Up and Let Go
○ Toss opened and expired items.
○ Recycle unfinished bottles, jars, rags, or towels.
○ Give away knickknacks, mismatched towel sets, and unused appliances.

Manage It Simply
Daily—Do a two-minute pickup of bathroom items each morning.
Weekly—Clean the sink, tub/shower, toilet, and floor.
Yearly—Reorganize the bathroom and linen closet, paint and decorate
as needed.

The bathroom can be a place of order and tranquility without much work.
Keep asking yourself, "What can I get rid of so I will always have a clean bathroom?" The goal is to eliminate clutter and have lots of clear space.

*Apply the "One-In, One-Out Rule," meaning if you bring anything new into
your collection, something old has to be removed at the same time. This is a great way
to warm up for a full-scale clutter cleanout—and learn basic control.*

—DON ASLETT

Simplify Your Active Space

Now that the visible and personal spaces of your life are simplified, it's time to branch off into more specific active spaces: the laundry room, your child's room, and the office. These busy spaces need systems within the system. There's a lot of daily activity going on in these rooms, but these spaces can still be under your control.

8

Simplify Your Laundry Room

Your decisions about laundry actually begin when you're purchasing your clothing. . . . A garment's label provides you with your first clue as to how difficult or expensive it will be to keep a garment clean and presentable.

—TOM MCNULTY

Everyone loves the feeling of throwing in a load of laundry and hearing the whirr of the washing machine. It makes you feel like you are really multitasking. But that's just the first step in our "same-day laundry principle" that will get your laundry back in the closet and drawers the same day you start it.

You need to take a look at your laundry space while you are getting those loads done. Your laundry space may be a separate room in your home, a small washer and dryer in a closet, or a spot in your basement or garage. The size of your laundry room doesn't matter; what matters is that the laundry gets done and the space stays clean.

To get your laundry room in shipshape order, we need to create an effective system that includes getting the laundry put away each day.

Create a Plan

An effective laundry system can help keep the rest of your house clean. Why? Because half-done laundry usually means overflowing laundry baskets in the family room, piles of dirty laundry on the floor to trip over, and folded laundry sitting on dressers to be put away.

No more laundry sitting out. Today it's possible to get it done, out of sight and out of mind, and enjoy a clean house knowing it's all put away.

With a simple setup and routine, you can definitely get your laundry room in working order in a short amount of time.

Here's the plan for simplifying your laundry space:

1. Finish the current laundry.
2. Obtain essential tools.
3. Set up a working laundry system.
4. Sort through your storage.

Simplify Your Laundry Room

Motivation:
- I'm tired of having overflowing laundry baskets around the house.
- I do laundry every day and want to do less.
- The laundry room should be easier to keep clean.

Supplies:
- Wastebasket and recycle bin for items to be discarded
- Donation box for items to be given away
- Clock to put on the wall

Time Estimate:
1–2 hours

Reward:
The satisfaction of knowing the laundry is done and the laundry room is clean.

Approach It by Sections

Begin by finishing your laundry. Households that need organizing often have laundry piles sitting out to be done. But this is an easy area to multitask and gain a sense of completion.

Each load of laundry involves four steps—wash, dry, fold, and put away. Chances are that there is generally one step that gets you bogged down, often the folding and putting away. But a successful laundry system enables you to get all four of those steps finished in one day.

Wash + Dry + Fold + Put Away = A Successful Laundry System!

When our older daughter was in sixth grade, she said, "Mom, you don't wash often enough." Before I got too upset, I asked, "What are you looking for?"

"My purple shirt," was her reply.

I reminded her that I just washed it two days before and led her to the washing machine. "It's time you learn to do your own laundry. I will give you one dollar for every load of laundry you do."

Her eyes lit up with glee, and I worried what I had done. But I recovered. "But you only get a dollar for every load that is washed, dried, folded, and put away the same day."

After only eight dollars, she came to me and said, "Mom, I like doing my laundry. You don't have to pay me anymore."

If a sixth grader can do it, you can do it too. Teach your family members to do their own laundry too. Work yourself out of a job and spend your time elsewhere.

How Long Does Laundry Take?

Here's the time involved for one load: half an hour to wash, half an hour to dry, and less than half an hour to fold and put clothes back in the drawers or closet.

One load = 1.5 hours
Two loads = 2 hours*
Three loads = 2.5 hours*

* This is based on the expectation that you keep adding a load to the washing machine right when you start the dryer, thereby moving the process ahead every thirty minutes.

The average person gets bogged down in folding and putting away. The solution? Use the next meal as leverage—you don't eat until the laundry is put away. You'll finish up quickly when you're hungry!

SPACE-SAVING TIP #22

Recognize where you get bogged down in completing the "same-day laundry system" of wash-dry-fold-put away, and finish the task the day you start.

Set Up Laundry with Essential Tools

Every laundry space is different, but you do need more tools than a washer and dryer. Be sure to include:

- *A laundry basket.* Find a hook on the wall or space on a nearby shelf to store the empty laundry basket so it doesn't become "homeless."
- *Laundry detergent and fabric softener.* Use up extra samples and minimize the detergent clutter.
- *A clock.* Most washer and dryer loads take less than thirty minutes, so hang a clock nearby and take note of when to return.
- *Lint box or wastebasket.* Clean the lint filter before each drying load to save electricity and to prevent a fire.
- *Clothes hamper(s).* Usually bedrooms stay cleaner if there is one in each bedroom closet or in the bathroom.
- *A sorting system.* You can sort by whites, darks, and lights. Or sort by whites, darks, blouses/shirts, and delicates.

Set Up a Working Laundry System

You can do laundry on an "as-needed basis." But if you do more than two loads a week, you will save time by having a weekly chart. For example:

Week at Home: Seven Loads of Laundry

MONDAY	TUESDAY	WEDNESDAY	THURSDAY	FRIDAY	SATURDAY	SUNDAY
Two loads: whites, towels	Two loads: darks, two sheet sets	X	One load: two more sheet sets	Two loads: whites, towels	X	X

1. Finish and Put Away Laundry
2. Set Up a Laundry System
3. Sort Storage Items

If you work from home, your weekends will be more pleasant if you get your laundry done during the week. And if you work outside the home, you can save time on the weekend by doing some loads during the week.

Working Week Away from Home: Seven Loads of Laundry

MONDAY	TUESDAY	WEDNESDAY	THURSDAY	FRIDAY	SATURDAY	SUNDAY
Two loads: whites, towels	X	X	Two loads: whites, darks	X	Three loads: towels and two loads of sheets	X

Spread the loads throughout the week so you don't have to do more than two or three at a time. This allows you time to get everything put away the same day.

SPACE-SAVING TIP #23

Leave the washing machine lid open to remind yourself to take out the last load of laundry from the dryer.

Clean Out Shelving and Cleaning Supplies

In a laundry space, there is usually at least one shelf for your detergent, spot remover, fabric softener, and lint box. But it can also become a spot for laundry samples, rags, missing buttons, and miscellaneous clutter. Simplify the space by clearing it off and storing items in matching baskets, especially unsightly but useful rags. Closed cabinets above the washer and dryer create a cleaner look in the space, though they still have to be cleaned out periodically.

SPACE-SAVING TIP #24

Save time ironing by folding clothes when they are still warm right out of the dryer.

A good ceiling light, a coat of paint, and pictures on the wall can turn a drab space into a pleasant place. When my family needed a new washer and dryer, my husband insisted he would go to the store and pick one out. "Not on your life, " I said. "I use the machine every day, so I need to like it."

When our college daughter came home, she said, "Oh, I see you picked the new washing machine, Mom."

"How do you know?" I asked.

"Because the handles are your favorite blue and green," she replied. She was exactly right. And I keep the tops of the washer and dryer clean because they're mine.

Whoever uses the space should decorate it to their tastes and make it a pleasant place.

Lighten Up and Let Go

One person needs to oversee the laundry to ensure that your clothes get folded and put away each day. Here are some tips that can make the job easier:

- Tina trained her children to put away their laundry by taping pictures inside the drawers of what went inside each drawer. They learned at an early age to put their laundry away.

- Marianne's high school son was extra busy with studies and sports and didn't have much time to do his own laundry. So she made a deal that if he started his wash Friday before school, she would dry and fold it. That gave him Friday and Saturday to put it away. The team system worked, and he learned that planning ahead for Friday mornings saved him half the work.

Laundry Room Checklist

____ 1. Do I know how many wash loads I do each week?

____ 2. Does my family get the dirty clothes in the hamper daily?

____ 3. Is my laundry basket near the washing machine or in a bedroom closet?

____ 4. Is a clock posted to keep the laundry moving forward every thirty minutes?

____ 5. Does the laundry get put away the same day it's started?

____ 6. Is there one laundry load that can be done every other week to save time?

____ 7. Have I cleaned out the laundry storage shelves in the last four months?

____ 8. Are the tops of the washer and dryer clear?

____ 9. Do I keep just the laundry supplies I need and actually use?

____ 10. Am I satisfied with my laundry space and system?

Tips from "The Decorating Coach," Susan Wells

Your work area need not reflect the dull routine of laundering. Paint the walls a favorite shade that you dare not use anywhere else! A warm color that complements the rest of your home will make up for the bland machines dominating the room.

Use open spaces as a background for inspiration. Have an office supply store copy photos of fun vacations, love notes from your children, or goofy teen poses. Choose one set of pictures, mount them onto a collection of inexpensive frames, and change the themes from time to time. You'll be entertained every time you enter.

Match the laundry baskets with low-cost storage bins, and your laundry room will no longer be the working "Cinderella" of the home.

Manage It Simply

The tops of the washer and dryer should always be as clear as your dining room table. Solve your space problems in the laundry room by asking what is not working and finding a solution.

One class participant said, "I used to put all my laundry away until I got a folding table." What's the obvious solution to that problem? Put away the folding table!

A safety tip to remember: don't ever leave home with the washer or dryer going. You need to be on hand in case a water hose leaks or the dryer catches on fire.

Review: The CALM Laundry Room Approach

Create a Plan
○ Finish the laundry.
○ Set up the laundry tools.
○ Chart a time system.

Approach It by Sections
○ Check that people are using clothes hampers and baskets.
○ Decide what is holding you back from finishing laundry the same day.
○ Analyze if your sorting system is working.

Lighten Up and Let Go
○ Lighten up by putting away the day's laundry.
○ Let go of time-consuming repairs of buttons and zippers.
○ Drop off dry cleaning early in the week and pick it up by Friday the same week.

Manage It Simply
Weekly—Wash as few days as possible, but get the laundry finished the same day you start it.
Biweekly—Look for loads of whites or other clothes you could do every other week, such as whites, jeans, or shirts.
Monthly—Review your weekly laundry chart and fine-tune it until it works well for you and your family.

The laundry room is probably the simplest space to organize yet the most cluttered room if it is out of control. With just a little time and attention, you can keep your laundry system in working order. Clear tops of the washer and dryer to show your job is done for the day.

The trouble with so many of us is that we underestimate the power of simplicity. We have a tendency it seems to overcomplicate our lives and forget what's important and what's not. We tend to mistake movement for achievement. We tend to focus on activities instead of results.

—ROBERT STUBERG

9

Simplify Your Child's Room

Divide and conquer. That's the best strategy for organizing a child's room.
Provide your child with enough containers of all sizes and shapes to sufficiently
hold their various belongings: one for the baseball cards, another for the rock
collection. Keep toys and games separate from legos and reading material.

—MAXINE ORDESKY

If you have children, you know that organizing a child's room is one of the most challenging aspects of simplifying your home. Why? Because you're dealing with a child (or teen) who is naturally flighty, busy, and distracted—and his or her room is used for sleeping, study, friends, and personal time.

One client took me to her teenage daughter's room and showed me what she saw every day—a "tornado" of clothes, toiletries, and piles of books and papers all over the room. After we talked through the five steps to organize this room, I noticed the teen's closet: it was completely empty except for four hangers with blouses on them. I thought, *You might as well give those away because she obviously doesn't like them. Everything she likes is on the floor, and everything she doesn't like is still hanging in the closet!*

In this chapter, we will look at simple ways you can help your child stay organized.

Create a Plan

The things in a child's room generally fall into one of three categories: clothes, books and papers, and toys, which are later replaced by sports equipment, music stands, and trophies or collections. You need to make each child's room consistent with his or her age. Otherwise, your kids may rebel at having baby or grade-school items still displayed when they are in junior high and high school.

Our plan consists of five steps to organizing a child's room. This should be done at least once a year, preferably before school starts. Pick a nonstressful time, such as when your child is out of school on the weekend or on a vacation day. Make it fun, and work together if your children are old enough.

Five steps to a clean room include:

1. Make the bed and clear the nightstand.
2. Clear the floor from the door to the bed.
3. Sort the room by three categories: clothes, paper, and toys.
4. Organize by sections: dresser, desk, and closet.
5. Set up paper and activity systems.

Simplify Your Child's Room

Motivation:

- I want my child to feel special.
- I want my child to benefit by being organized at home.
- I want the room to reflect my child and his or her achievements.

Supplies:

- Wastebasket and recycle bin for items to be discarded
- Clothes hamper
- Labels for drawers, shelves, and boxes
- Notepad with listed categories: "To Do," "To Buy," "Next Steps"
- A memory book consisting of a three-ring binder, sheet protectors, and tabbed dividers
- A nice memory box that fits in the closet

Time Estimate:

2–4 hours (depending on the condition of the room and collections needing organizing)

Reward:
A sense of order and appreciation so your child can succeed at school and face life with confidence.

Approach It by Sections

Five easy steps will get your child's room in shape in no time. Whether you are just tidying up on the weekend or doing a seasonal cleanup, these are the steps to follow.

Bed and Nightstand

Start by making the bed, and 50 to 70 percent of the room will look clean immediately.

Determine what day and how often you plan to change the sheets. Weekly or every two weeks is normal. By fourth grade, most kids can pull off their sheets and put them in the laundry on the day you specify, though they may need help putting them back on the bed. Use a sheet and a comforter to make it simple for your child to make his own bed. The fewer layers of bedding, the better the chance your child will succeed at making his own bed.

It is useful to have a reading light attached to the headboard or on the nightstand so your child can turn it off without getting out of bed. A nightstand or bookshelf beside the bed should hold your child's books, clock, and CD player to allow him to unwind at night. Also, I suggest that you place a comfortable chair somewhere in the room, so you can sit and talk or read to them at night. Your children will likely talk to you more at night than at any other time.

Floor

The next largest surface to clear up is the floor. Stand at the doorway and help your child clear a path to the bed (if things are in bad shape). Then clear the rest of the floor to the closet and to the desk. Soon it should be back to its normal state—nothing on the floor except furniture!

With a young child, you can play "Magic Pickup." Everything that needs to be put away is put on the made bed. Then you ask, "Is this clothes, a book, or a toy?" Once the child identifies the category, ask where that goes and put it up together.

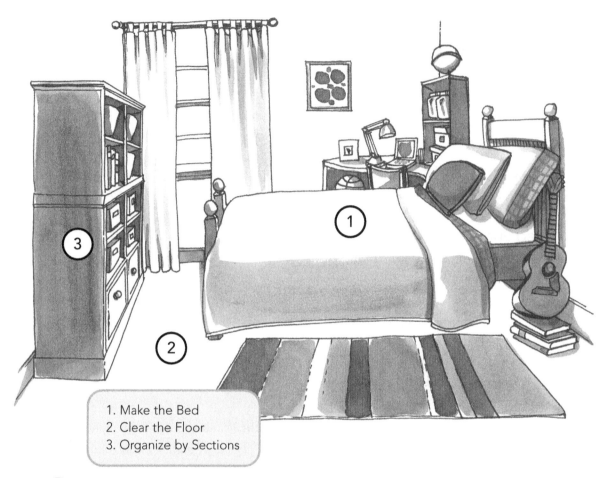

1. Make the Bed
2. Clear the Floor
3. Organize by Sections

 SPACE-SAVING TIP #25

Children are natural collectors, so help them display their favorite items on a dresser or shelf to show you are proud of them.

Clothes, Paper, and Toys

Clean clothes get hung up or put in a drawer, and dirty clothes go in the hamper. Put a clothes hamper in or near the closet to minimize piles of clothes on the floor.

Books go on a bookshelf with the spines lined up neatly with a straight edge. Papers go into binders or two-pocket folders at the desk or on a bookshelf. You can keep a three-hole punch in their room if you want them to place their papers in school binders.

Store sentimental or significant papers in a memory book—a three-ring binder that holds these papers in sheet protectors, sorted by grade level. Keep papers your children are particularly proud of or ones that represent their daily work. As mentioned earlier, your child's papers, awards, and photos from birth through high school can be stored in approximately four memory books.

Toys go on shelves with the largest ones on the bottom, medium ones in the middle, and small toys like blocks or Barbie accessories in boxes or trays on the top shelf. As the child grows, the toys on these shelves will be replaced with collections, memorabilia, framed pictures, and trophies.

> **SPACE-SAVING TIP #26**
>
> Create a three-ring memory book with sheet protectors and tabbed grade-level dividers to hold special papers, awards, report cards, and photos.

Dresser and Closet

Now that the visible space is organized, it's time to get inside the cabinets and closet. Get the bed made and floor clean first so you have clear space to work.

Start with the top dresser drawer and work downward. Each drawer should hold clothes with a similar theme, like play clothes, school clothes, pants, tops, or underwear. The drawer that is waist-high for your child should be the one he accesses daily. Top drawers should be divided with shoeboxes or jewelry boxes for small items like hair barrettes, jewelry, and keys. Bottom drawers hold larger items that are less used, like winter clothes, sweaters, and blankets.

Next, work on the closet. A child's closet is important and relatively easy to organize if you adjust it to his needs. If he has a lot of toys, put them in shelves on one side. If your child is young, hang a lower bar so he can reach his hanging clothes. Install shelving up to the top of the closet if you need room to store an extra set of bedsheets, out-of-season clothes, and his memory box.

Remember, a child's closet doesn't just have to be for clothes. It can store toys, sports equipment, and laundry hamper. You can arrange your child's hanging clothes by categories or organize them by outfits to make it easier for your child to dress himself.

SPACE-SAVING TIP #27

The best motivator for your child to clean up at any age is you! Ten minutes of your full attention and help will result in progress faster than hours of you nagging from another room.

Desk

A desk in the child's room is a good place to organize his study time, even if your child seems prone to study at the kitchen table. But if your child studies in his room, it is important to have these items: a good reading light, a clear work surface, and a computer, depending on his age.

Follow the plan in chapter 10 for setting up the desk. Be sure to have drawers with a desk tray for their supplies plus a file drawer for folders and a space for binders. An easy way to keep papers until you have time to sort them is in a magazine holder. On the weekend, put them in file folders or into tabbed sections of the binder.

Be sure your child is not carrying excess weight to school with too many books and binders. Keep a binder for completed papers at home and arrange completed papers with the most recent paper on top in front. Label the front and spine of the binder with the subject.

Your children will have a better chance of succeeding at school if you regularly help them keep their room and papers in order for school. Some children need more help than others. Meet the needs of your child. Even in the same family, each one is different.

Lighten Up and Let Go

A child's room needs continual sorting, so keep it fun and keep at it. Your child's room is his retreat from the world and a place you can show him you care about him.

Child's Room Checklist

_____ 1. Is the bed easy to make with a reading lamp nearby?

_____ 2. Is the floor picked up each night before bed?

_____ 3. Do all my child's clothes fit in the closet and dresser drawers with easy access?

_____ 4. Is there a place to study and a place for my child's backpack and schoolbooks?

_____ 5. Do I have a memory book to organize my child's best work, awards, and photos?

_____ 6. Do the toys all fit on shelves, or do I need to put some away for a while?

_____ 7. Is the closet rod organized and items organized on the floor and shelves?

_____ 8. Is my child's desk set up with light, supplies, and clear space?

_____ 9. Have I given away unworn clothes and outgrown toys and books in the past four months?

_____ 10. Is the room well organized and meeting my child's needs for sleep, dressing, and study?

Tips from "The Decorating Coach," Susan Wells

Walls serve as the perfect springboard to showcase your child's individuality. If your child's favorite color is too bold for the room, compromise by painting accents like shelving or furniture.

Transform a corkboard into a unique backdrop for artwork or photos. Glue fabric around the cork that matches the bedding. Frame with two-inch molding, and it will become a focal point.

Showcase your child's interests with displays that also add storage. A shelf hung above the window or doorframe could hold a collection of trains or dolls. Paint the shelving and frame the same shade to become a unique architectural unit. Let your child add dollops of crazy color with pillows or baskets, and you'll go from bedroom to dream room.

Manage It Simply

A child's room needs to grow to reflect his age. Usually, organizing your children's clothes before school starts in the fall and with the seasonal changes is adequate. On holidays, catch up on sorting toys or paperwork. Go through papers and tidy up the room for a fresh start to each school week on the weekends.

- Paul complained to his mother, "Mom, I have no socks." She dismissed the continuing comments because she knew there was a drawer full of socks in his room. But one morning when she heard it again from her preschooler, she pulled out the drawer and the two sat on the floor as she held up each pair. The repeated response? "Those hurt, Mom." And she promptly put them in a donations bag. When they finished going through the drawer, it was empty. He looked up at her and said, "See, I have no socks!" He was right.

- Gaby was in junior high and fairly organized, but her dresser drawers were never closed. I held up each piece of clean clothing and asked two questions, "Do you like this? Do you wear it?"

    When the answer was "no" to either question, we put it in our donations pile. She had emotionally outgrown several items now that she was going into high school. The final outcome was she gave away thirteen items and all the clothes fit in the dresser. She then kept the dresser drawers closed.

- Jessica was a senior in high school when I went to organize her room. She and her best friend had gotten ready that morning for my visit. "What are these eight trash bags outside your door?" I asked.

    Her friend spoke up. "We got ready for you by bagging up all the clothes on the floor. That's just her dirty laundry, and she usually has about two feet of clothes all over the floor." That was a lot of clothes!

    We were going to start the laundry while we worked but discovered it hadn't been sorted. The solution? Her friend taught her how to sort lights, darks, and delicates. Later Jessica's mom bought her one big white hamper for whites and an equally large hamper for darks. Problem solved. She just needed laundry baskets and Saturday washdays to keep her room clean and neat.

Review: The CALM Child's Room Approach

Create a Plan
○ Make the bed and clean the nightstand.
○ Clear the floor and organize dresser surfaces.
○ Organize by sections: sleep, dressing, play, and study.

Approach It by Sections
○ Organize the closet by hanging clothes, floor, and shelves.
○ Sort each drawer and shelf one at a time.
○ Set up the desk with everything your child needs to succeed.

Lighten Up and Let Go
○ Clothes to friends' children or to a charity.
○ Toys, stuffed animals to charity or on the top shelf of the closet.
○ Books donated to the library.

Manage It Simply
Daily—Spend fifteen minutes with your child before bedtime putting away items and preparing for the next day.

Weekly—On the weekends, make sure laundry is caught up, assignments for the coming week are on the child's calendar, and homework bag is emptied and papers in order for the coming week.

Seasonally—Go through your child's closet and drawers to weed out outgrown items and replace with new ones.

When you help your children simplify their rooms, it teaches them skills that last for a lifetime and improves their academic success. My motto as a parent and former teacher is, when children learn to work orderly, they learn to think orderly.

To make sure you get everything, begin with the area to the left side of your bedroom door and work around the entire room.

—JOY BERRY

10

Simplify Your Office

Think of yourself as an air traffic controller and your desktop as the runway.
You're in charge. You determine which papers, piles, and projects
can land on your desk—and stay there.

—SUSAN SILVER

The one room in your home you most need to organize to stay on top of your life is your office. Yet this room can be the place where you feel the most overwhelmed by paper, projects, and e-mails.

It doesn't have to be that way. Though you may have many demands on your time and attention, there are ways to get your workspace in order and move through your workload more smoothly. The organizing principles are similar whether your office area is a small desk, a computer station, or an entire office you work in eight hours a day. The goal is the same: putting you comfortably back in control of your organized office space.

Often, the problem is your office has outgrown what worked before. You have too much input plus too much backlog, and suddenly the space is out of control.

Create a Plan

Stand back and survey your office space. Is it cluttered by paper, books, or projects spilling over onto the floor? If it is overflowing in any spot, there's too much stuff and not enough space. It's time to dig in and arrange things to work for you, not against you. It's time to catch up and simplify your workspace.

This chapter will follow a specific order for efficient sorting. I'll also include time tips to maintain each area too.

1. List the changes you want in your office space.
2. Clear the desk top and clean the supply drawers.
3. Deal with the piles on flat surfaces and the floor.
4. Weed out your files and file drawers.
5. Simplify storage cabinets.
6. Simplify your e-mail.
7. List your goals and inspirational thoughts.

Simplify Your Office

Motivation:
- I'm tired of wasting time looking for things.
- I don't want to feel stressed when walking into my office.
- I want a professional image, and my office needs to improve.

Supplies:
- Office supplies: paper clips, stapler, sticky notes, notepad
- File folders and labels (or label maker)
- Personal goals for the next three months
- Recycle bin and shredder

Time Estimate:
4–6 hours for the space, plus 2–4 hours per file drawer

Reward:
An organized office ready to step into and use anytime.

Approach It by Sections

There is no better way to simplify your office than by sections. Complete one section successfully, and soon you will double your productivity and put your mind at ease.

List Desired Changes

First, list the changes you want in this space. It is important to make a list of your desired changes so you can see the benefits ahead. Potential changes include:

- Find daily project files quickly
- Have all the bills to pay in one spot
- Get rid of all the paper piles
- Locate things you need right away
- Have evening free time
- Send a thank-you note within twenty-four hours
- Get off the computer and on with your life

I believe every office problem has a simple solution. So let's identify some common problems and then look at practical ways to solve them.

Desktop and Supply Drawers

The first step in simplifying your office is to clean up the desktop and supply drawers. Create a clear center space by stacking papers neatly on one side. Corral all sticky notes and business cards into a small box. Now clean the desk itself with a dust rag, sponge, or window cleaner.

Place the contents of the supply drawer on top of the desk and then clean the drawer. Now carefully put back office supplies you absolutely need in the desk tray divider. Get rid of the rest. If your desk doesn't have a supply drawer, then use a desktop supply holder.

Place an imaginary horizontal line midway across your desk or surface. The half closest to you is the inner workspace, while the back half is called the outer workspace. The space closest to you is where you work and should only contain one pile of the active incoming work each day on the side where you enter and sit down.

The outer section of your desk houses your phone, computer, lamp, and outgoing corner (or in-box). Don't start a pile or stash any papers in that area! Instead, keep them in your inner space.

SPACE-SAVING TIP #28

You will accomplish more if you work from a written to-do list assigning times to accomplish each item today, tomorrow, and the next day.

Once your supplies are arranged, you are ready to sort your desktop papers. Get a notepad or open a blank page on your computer to create a master list of work you need to do. Then assign each task you uncover on your desk to the three days you can most control: today, tomorrow, and the next day. List high priority items at the top.

Once you have listed the tasks on your three-day list or your master to-do list, you may be tempted to jump in and start taking care of the items right away. You may do that if your list of things to do on your desktop has created anxiety and concern. But don't start until you list everything on the desktop.

Three-Day To-Do List

TODAY (MONDAY)	TUESDAY	WEDNESDAY
___ Order business cards	___ Mail package	___ Call for dr. appt.
___ Write proposal	___ Draft cover letter	___ Mail proposal
___ Pay bills	___ Get airline tickets	___ Line up event speaker
___ Sort in-box	___ Send thank-you note	___ E-mail new client
___ RSVP party	___ Deposit checks	___ Sort client files

Master To-Do List

___ Clarify 401(k) withdrawal amount

___ Get health insurance straightened out

___ Pay off and cancel store credit card

___ Buy new planner and pages

Desk Setup

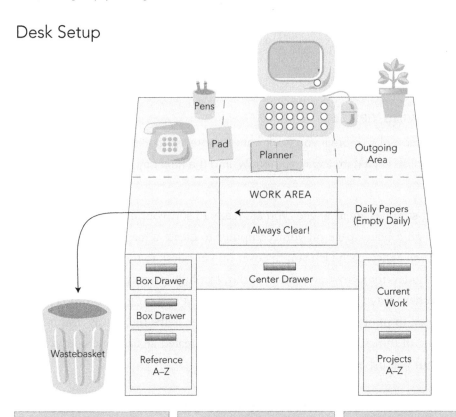

ON YOUR DESK	CENTER DRAWER	BOX DRAWER

1. Telephone
2. Pad of Paper
3. Pen Location
4. Planner
5. Clock
6. Incoming Corner/
   Outgoing Area
7. Plant or 10" Picture
	1. Large and Small
	   Paper Clips
	2. Rubber Bands
	3. Post-It Notes
	4. Removable Tape
	5. Ruler
	6. Scissors
	7. Letter Opener
		1. Envelopes (2 sizes)
		2. 3 x 5 Cards
		3. Computer Disks
		4. Receipts, Checkbook
		5. Stationery Notes
		6. Phone Messages
		7. Personal Items

TIME	DECISIVENESS	CATCH UP
20–25 minutes daily, or 2 hours per week. Develop a regular daily habit.	Narrow down to the two best choices. Move the paper to the next step.	Start from today forward! Then deal with the backlog.

1. Organize Desktop
2. Set Up Supplies
3. Weed Out File Drawers

SPACE-SAVING TIP #29

To sort papers more quickly, start at the back of a file or the bottom of your in-box. Older papers are easier to toss than recent ones.

Flat Surfaces and Floor

After you have simplified your desktop and supply drawers, it is time to deal with the piles on the flat surfaces and the floor of your office. Less important work is often piled on the floor, shelves, or credenza, waiting for the "right time" to get finished. Let's deal with these piles now.

Check your three-day to-do list and place in your in-box any items that need to be packaged and mailed, returned, fixed, or researched for an upcoming project.

As you go through the rest of the piles, ask yourself, "If I don't do it this week, when am I going to do it?" Be decisive! Assign it to a specific calendar date end time, or move it onto the Master to-do list.

If you are procrastinating on a certain paperwork project, it's probably because you have to find the receipt, package the item in the right size box, fill out the mailing label, go to the post office, and stand in line to get postage. The process seems so overwhelming. To reduce your stress and increase your likelihood of success, list only the next step on your to-do list. That way, you will stop procrastinating and get the return project in motion, one step at a time.

SPACE-SAVING TIP #30

Sort your paperwork by asking, "Is this paper worth my time and space to deal with it?" If the answer is no, let it go. If the answer is yes, get it done as soon as possible.

Files and File Drawers

The next step in simplifying your office space is to weed out your files and file drawers. Label each file drawer with the main one or two categories. Allow room at the front of one file drawer to include projects you are currently working on.

Begin at the back of each file drawer and pull out ten inches of papers. Place these papers on your clear desktop, line up the recycle bin to your left, and start sorting. As you view each file or paper, ask yourself these two questions:

1. Is this file or paper part of my present and future work?
2. Do I need to keep this file or paper, or is it time to pitch it?

Here are some tips to speed up the process of simplifying your files:

- Stand and get into a toss rhythm
- Have a decisive person work with you
- Postpone eating dinner until you finish
- Limit the file sort time to two hours
- Plan a big reward for completing your files in the time allotted

After you have sorted through your existing files, create files for loose papers that seem to accumulate. Be sure to include the following files in your system:

   ___ "New Contacts": a file in which to place information for new contacts. Enter these once a week, or delegate them to an assistant.

   ___ "New Topics": a file in which to place information related to new topics, such as a new project, a new client, or a new interest.

   ___ "Three-Day To-Do List": a file in which to place papers that correspond with action items on your three-day to-do list.

A thirty-one-day file with accordion slots lets you put a paper in on the day you are going to deal with it. This only works if you are disciplined to do it on that day.

Daily Mail

The average household receives fifteen pieces of mail a day: five are junk mail that can be recycled, five are important bills that can be filed, and the remaining five often start a clutter pile.

You can get your daily mail pile under control by creating a personal organizing center and using or adapting the five-file-folder system described in chapter 4.

Storage Cabinets

Next, sort your storage cabinets by shelf. Empty one shelf's contents onto your clear desktop, wipe down the shelf, and then replace only what you use for your work. Or place items in three piles: keep, maybe keep, and toss. Then put back what you decide to keep, and only put half of the "maybe keeps" back. The more you toss, the better.

Sometimes it's hard to let go of neatly organized items because they are so tightly compacted. Don't let an efficient storage bin stop you from purging unnecessary paperwork!

Do one wall, then the next until you have gone through it all and you are satisfied you are storing the things current to your business.

E-mail

Cut down on your office stress by simplifying your e-mail. Take a moment to evaluate your e-mail system. Do you respond within four hours, and are you keeping an uncluttered inbox? Also, estimate how much time you spend checking and replying to e-mail, compare it to the time you spend accomplishing your daily to-do list, and determine if it is in proper balance for your job. Most jobs require prompt e-mail responses, but there are usually other things to get finished.

Some people make the mistake of using their e-mail as their to-do list. Clear out your e-mail inbox for the day by responding to e-mails and creating e-mail file folders. Leave only the e-mails needing your response in your inbox, and move the rest of them off the screen to these files.

Each Friday, review your e-mail files and delete any unnecessary e-mails.

Personal Goals

To stay focused as you work, make a list of short-term and long-term goals, and post them in an easily visible space. For example, you can write your goals on an index card, insert it in an easy-to-open frame, and place it on your desk next to your computer.

When writing your goals, be sure to state them in the present, such as, "I am living my dream making a difference at work and raising my family. At home my goal is to sort my mail into five folders every day, reply to e-mails in the same day, and leave my desk with a three-day to-do list on my clutter-free desktop."

Lighten Up and Let Go

Simplify your office space by working toward your stated goals, letting go of tasks that do not match those goals, and creating systems to solve problems. For example, clear out an easily accessible file drawer to hold excess desktop items or useful project files you reach for often.

Anything that doesn't support your daily needs should be stored away from your desk. You should go through long-term storage items regularly and recycle or give away items you no longer need.

Office Checklist

_____ 1. Have I created a list of the main things I want to change about my workspace?

_____ 2. Is my desktop organized and clutter free?

____ 3. Do I have a three-day to-do list and master project list?

____ 4. Could anyone walk into my office and find a pen and notepad?

____ 5. Can I eliminate a pile this week to clean up my area?

____ 6. Have I sorted and tossed files in the last three months?

____ 7. Do I regularly give away unused items from storage shelves or drawers?

____ 8. Do I respond within four hours to e-mail while working off my to-do list?

____ 9. Have I posted a list of goals that reflect my work focus?

____ 10. Do I enjoy my work area and accomplish my work comfortably?

Tips from "The Decorating Coach," Susan Wells

A home office can be functional yet fantastic! Choose the basics that are hardest to acquire first, such as patterned fabric for furniture or drapery, plain carpet next, and paint last. Flat surfaces in the room can be softened by texture and tapestries, such as a wool wall hanging, a stone sculpture, or a succulent plant to brighten a bare corner.

The wood finishes of the bookcase, desk, flooring, or blinds must either be repeated in more than one piece, or complement one another (a lighter grain contrasting a darker shade, similar tones highlighting the same color). Since too many wood grains can detract from the harmony of the room, it's best to incorporate no more than two.

Complete your work area with elements that inspire: a photo of a mentor, a plaque inscribed with your favorite proverb, a framed thank-you note, or a favorite possession that reflects your passions.

Manage It Simply

The key to maintaining an organized office is to develop the habit of getting your work done and filed at the end of each day. Keep your paperwork simple to get more done.

Another factor is that clean offices have empty wastebaskets. Why? Empty wastebaskets encourage staff (and family) to get rid of old paper and recycle often.

- Diane's home office space consisted of a computer table tucked in the corner of her living room, behind the wall of her entryway. This setup should have worked, except she also did paperwork for her kids there . . . and in the kitchen . . . and in an upstairs bedroom. Paperwork drifted to the dining room table, and soon the office clutter was out of control.

  We tucked a two-drawer file into the corner of the nearby dining room and used it as a serving piece. She filed the dining room papers there, all home papers went upstairs to the office, and she carried her work to the computer when she brought it home. Ideally all of her office paperwork should be in one room, but Diane preferred the change of pace by moving back and forth.

- One school principal was so busy with district meetings, parents dropping in, faculty questions, and students needing special attention that organizing her office was at the bottom of her list.

  Mary's morale was suffering, as was her workload, until we spent a spring vacation day going through her office. We listed her desired changes and tasks, and then we sorted and filed the piles of paperwork in appropriate file drawers. The next day, Mary was back in control when the first teacher showed up in her office. Her staff was very impressed and more respectful.

- After organizing one cubicle office, my client successfully tossed seven large garbage bags of paperwork. When we finished getting rid of his old files and stacks of unneeded papers, he said, "I forgot. I have a five-drawer lateral file in the hallway. Do you think we should do that too?"

  Of course! Everything you own pertaining to your office should be sorted at the same time. Since he was still motivated to simplify his office, we plowed through the lateral file in short order. He postponed dinner, but the extra time was worth it to complete the entire task. We were both relieved when the task was finished.

Review: The CALM Office Approach

Create a Plan
○ Sort your desktop and computer area.
○ Organize your supplies.
○ List work on a three-day to-do list and master to-do list.

Approach It by Sections
○ Eliminate piles until they are all gone.
○ Weed out your file drawers one at a time.
○ Go through storage areas and keep current items.

Lighten Up and Let Go
○ Throw away or recycle old papers whenever you open a file drawer.
○ Keep current and future files, but toss files for past projects no longer needed.
○ Store important historical papers out of your daily reach.

Manage It Simply
Daily—Clean your desk, sort your e-mail, and review your three-day to-do list.
Weekly—Sort your e-mail folders each Friday and review your master to-do list.
Monthly—Update your quarterly goals and improve one system in your office to save even more time.

No matter how overwhelming the task may seem, you can simplify your office one section at a time. Once you create a system that works, you will minimize your piles, files, and crises as you become more decisive about what works for you.

Respect the law of in-boxes: They put it in, you take it out, and if you don't recycle or refer it, you identify the action you're going to take, then put it in a safe home and post a note on a list in your calendar.

—PORTER KNIGHT

Simplify Your Formal Space

These three "formal" rooms in your home are spaces for your family and your guests to enjoy. Though simplifying these rooms may not take long, you will be pleased when they remain the same organized way you leave them. Let's examine each of these rooms to make sure they contain things you currently need and appreciate.

11

Simplify Your Dining Room

Sometimes entertaining is not fun because we have unrealistic expectations
about what we need to do. The watchword is "simplify."

—KATHLEEN KENDALL-TACKETT

If your home has a dining room, you may enjoy special dinner parties, evenings, and lively conversations over turkey dinner at Thanksgiving and Christmas. But the rest of the year, the dining room often becomes a window dressing room—admired but untouched. Other times, it becomes a catchall for homework, travel planning, or unfinished sewing projects.

Let's take a good look at your dining room and make sure it is in good shape—no clutter hanging around that should be moved on. In this chapter, we will learn how to deal with tablecloths, finer pieces of china, and where to put everything associated with decorating your table.

Create a Plan

The dining room has an easy-to-follow plan that we will use in the remaining rooms of your home. If in doubt about your dining room, follow this overall plan for simplifying your space.

1. The dining table and chairs should be cleared.
2. The floor should be cleared in a clockwise fashion, including piles tucked in a corner or under a china cabinet.
3. Sort the china cabinet, hutch, and sideboard from the top down, one shelf and one drawer at a time.
4. Decide where you will store tablecloths, silver, china, and centerpieces neatly.

Simplify Your Dining Room

Motivation:
- Company's coming!
- I'd like to have a nice, clean area to entertain guests and make my family feel special.
- I want to clear off the dining room table.

Supplies:
- Dust cloths and furniture polish
- Vacuum
- Three boxes for things to put away, donate, and sell

Time Estimate:
3–4 hours

Reward:
An attractive room that is always ready for company or a family dinner.

When simplifying your dining room, avoid the pitfall of pulling out items and not making same-day decisions whether to put an item back or pass it on to another family member. If that happens, take a picture of the item, put it back, and then deal with it in the "Lighten Up and Let Go" section of this chapter.

Approach It by Sections

To follow the plan for your dining room, just do one step at a time. Soon the room will be ready to use and easier to clean up.

Dining Table and Chairs

First, the dining table and chairs need to be cleared of clutter. If there are things on your table that shouldn't be there, the best way to do this is to go in a clockwise fashion and put away each pile.

- Daily papers and bills go to your personal organizing center or home office.
- Newspapers go to the recycle bin.
- School projects go in your child's room or backpack to return to school.
- Serving pieces should be polished and put away.

Keep the dining room table clear, and you will have one less room to pick up. Push in the chairs to keep piles from starting there as well.

SPACE-SAVING TIP #31

Use the ten-minute rule for clearing your dining table: put everything away ten minutes after using the table so no clutter lingers.

Floor

After the table is clean, the floor should next be cleared and cleaned. This would seem obvious, but many times busyness and visual tune out keep us from noticing a dirty floor.

Piles on your dining room floor may have accumulated from a photo project that you started with enthusiasm but never finished. Place these photo supplies in a labeled box and put it away. Pick a holiday or schedule evenings to catch up. The process of clearing piles from your floors usually is rewarding once you get started and takes less time than you think.

After a party or celebration, be sure to mop or vacuum the floor thoroughly. You don't want stains or food to linger and spot your flooring. Cleanup is easier within twenty-four hours.

1. Clear Dining Room Table
2. Clean the Floor
3. Sort China Cabinet

SPACE-SAVING TIP #32

A china cabinet is a good place to display special objects and keep your china sets dust free and ready to use. Thin out unused items so your cabinet stays beautiful and simple.

China Cabinet and Hutch

Sort your china cabinet or hutch with a top-down approach. Empty the first shelf onto the table into three sections: things you want to keep, things you maybe want to keep, and things to give away. Focus on keeping the useful and attractive favorite sets. Let go of unmatched pieces.

Clean out the display shelves by dusting or waxing. Now put back the "keep" items. Does your shelf look better with just those items? If so, consider where else you could store or give away items.

Empty one shelf and drawer, sorting into "keep" and "giveaway" items. By the end of the process you may have some valuables that you don't want to return to your collection. What should you do with these?

Family Valuables

Valuables in the dining room that you have outgrown can be given away to various places. For example, pass along some of your "family keepsakes." Offer these items to relatives of the original owner of the china or silver you are ready to pass on. If they aren't interested, offer them to younger nieces and nephews who may be thrilled to have a part of your family history.

If none of your relatives are interested in the items, offer them to an antique dealer or estate sale service. You can also sell these pieces through local auctions or online through eBay or Craigslist.

SPACE-SAVING TIP #33

Be ready to entertain guests by keeping a "household" notebook that lists the size and setting of your tablecloths, serving pieces, and meals for various numbers of guests.

Storage

Next, consider your storage areas of dining room tablecloths, silver, china, and centerpieces. Now is the time to also make a list of items you have stored elsewhere that relate to dining or holiday celebrations.

- *Tablecloths*. Iron and then neatly fold your tablecloths over a hanger and store in a closet from smallest to largest, or fold them in a dining room hutch drawer.
- *Napkins*. Keep napkins wrinkle free by putting them in a shallow gift box in a dining room or kitchen cabinet. Include the napkin ring holders.
- *Silver*. Keep good silver in a velvet-lined case or another divided tray so it won't scratch. Simplify by having matched numbers of silverware and place settings.
- *Serving pieces*. Sort and keep your favorite sets of silver and china serving pieces. Keep silver from tarnishing in a china cabinet or sealed plastic bag.
- *Large serving platters*. Large platters take creativity to store either by hanging them, putting them in a china cabinet, or hiding them under a sofa. If you don't use them regularly, pass them on.
- *Centerpieces*. Evaluate each centerpiece to see if you still like it and if you have room to store all of them. Store candles in a cooler place, and don't keep more than you need.

Lighten Up and Let Go

During the process of simplifying your dining room, you sorted items into those you want to keep, maybe keep, and those you are ready to let go. The challenge is to not pile the "let go" items into a corner like an unfinished project. Here are some ideas to help you narrow down the process and give yourself deadlines for letting go of these items.

Take a picture of all the items you are willing to pass on. Ask relatives if they are interested in these family items. If so, they will be happy to have these items, and you will be happy to give the item a new home and free up space in your dining room.

Find local antique shops, consignment shops, or an estate sale company. Be sure to get estimates from two to three different places before parting with the items.

Use Internet services such as eBay or Craigslist to find a broader base of potential buyers or services. There are plenty of eBay dealers who will help you sell your items for a percentage of the sale. Just be willing to price and ship it, or have it purchased and picked up locally.

Be encouraged that you are doing yourself and your family a favor by clearing out valuable things now. Though it is a project in itself, visualize a sparkling dinner table with your friends and family in a clutter-free room.

Dining Room Checklist

____ 1. Is the dining room table clear with an attractive centerpiece?

____ 2. Is the floor clean and free of piles?

____ 3. Have I cleaned out the china cabinet and hutch in the last year?

____ 4. Are my special pieces displayed and easy to maintain?

____ 5. Have I passed on the family keepsakes I have outgrown?

____ 6. Do I have organized storage of all my table accessories?

____ 7. Have I finished all the projects stored in the dining room?

____ 8. Have I thinned out the dining room centerpieces, silver, and china?

____ 9. Have I created good memories of family and friends in here?

____ 10. Is the dining room attractive and useful for my lifestyle now?

Tips from "The Decorating Coach," Susan Wells

The dining room table holds the key to creating the room's ambience. Center a group of pillar candles in a glass tray or low bowl. Line with decorative stones for textural interest. Occasionally, pour water over the stones and float seasonal flowers. In the fall, envelop orange candles with small gourds and pumpkins.

Lend a flair for the holidays by removing the stones and augmenting red candles with miniature tree ornaments. Liven the collection for spring by setting the dish over purple fabric falling in rich folds. Tint water with food coloring and adorn with white candles, stones, and lilies.

Along the length of the table, repeat small replicas of the centerpiece. Farewell to boring settings—your creative touch has made the gathering of friends and family a heartwarming event!

Manage It Simply

Some people have an easier time than others using dining space. But maintaining an attractive, useable dining room can be easy if you have a plan.

- Diane found piles of clutter on her dining room from shopping trips and children's memory books that she intended to get to. Once we spent a few hours clearing the accumulated clutter, we put on a tablecloth and centerpiece that was too formal to stack bags or projects on. The result? Clutter piles drastically diminished, and her clean dining room was a big plus in giving guests the overall impression of a clean home.

- My family's dining room is ready to host various events with five table leaves to expand the table. However, the room wasn't getting much use except for guests and holidays.

  We now either eat in the dining room on Friday night to celebrate the accomplishments of the week, or we use our good china and a candle in the kitchen to have that same special feeling. With dimmed lights and soft background music, it's cheaper than going out to eat and allows us to relax and talk before the weekend activities.

- Audrey was dating a wonderful man, but every time she was invited to eat at his place, he had to clear the table and chairs of all his paper piles. She was considering marrying him, but she was hesitant because of the perpetual clutter.

  A word to the wise: even your relationships can be hampered by your habits. Opposites do attract, but you should "step up" your organization for company and in common areas. It can be done with a little more preparation and attention to the space.

Review: The CALM Dining Room Approach

Create a Plan

○ The dining table and chairs should be attractive.

○ The floor should be clutter free and clean.

○ China cabinets and storage items need to be sorted.

Approach It by Sections

○ Each shelf and drawer should be emptied one at a time.

○ Sort through your centerpieces and tablecloths.

○ Make sure you have matching numbers of silverware and place settings.

Lighten Up and Let Go

○ Offer family keepsakes to relatives to enjoy.

○ Find local shops to sell or consign your items.

○ Use Internet services to find a buyer for your items.

Manage It Simply

Daily—Keep a nice tablecloth and centerpiece on your dining table so it is less tempting to put clutter there.

Monthly/Holidays—Keep the dining space under control by going through it monthly if you host guests often, or before the holidays.

Seasonally—Polish the wood and dust the china cabinet.

The dining room can stay relatively clean if you put things back after each use. Find a beautiful centerpiece and enjoy this place of order and simplicity.

Before scheduling anything into your calendar for the week, begin by filling in 30 minutes of organizing time each day. Since you're making an organizing appointment, you're indicating that doing so is just as important to you as your other scheduled appointments.

—MARIA GRACIA

12

Simplify Your
Living Room

Where do people literally live anyway? When we are at home, studies show,
approximately 96 percent of our time is spent alone or with our family—but only
four percent of that home time is spent in company. This is all the more reason
to create a living room that you will really put to use.

—ALEXANDRA STODDARD

One room that can expand your living space is your living room. Depending on how you envision the space, this room can be a quiet spot to read, a place to look at favorite photos, or a cozy place to talk with your spouse or kids.

The living room is probably the most formal room in your home, likely somewhere near your front entry. Your living room should be one of your more beautiful, clutter free rooms. And if your family room and living room are the same, that is even more important because now guests and family share the same space.

The name "living room" can be a misnomer in that often not much actual living happens there. You may keep it strictly for entertaining on formal occasions, or you may have added a computer desk or piano to allow daily activity to happen there.

Decide what purpose you would like this room to serve at this time in your life, and then review the practical tips in this chapter to help you plan the space to become a "living" room that serves you.

Create a Plan

Our goal is to clean, simplify, and arrange your living room space to meet your current needs.

The plan consists of three steps:

1. Dust and polish tabletops in the room.
2. Organize cabinets and stored items.
3. Fine-tune the room by activity zones.

Simplify Your Living Room

Motivation:
- This could be a great reading space.
- I want my living room to be a nice space for family and friends.
- It's pretty simple to maintain once it's in order.

Supplies:
- Dust cloth and furniture polish
- Vacuum
- Three boxes for things to put away, donate, and sell

Time Estimate:
2–4 hours

Reward:
A living room you can use for reading, relaxing, and entertaining.

Approach It by Sections

Sit in your living room and make a list of the activities that happen in this room. Would a lamp by each chair invite you to relax and read a magazine here? Does someone play the piano or clarinet here? Do you sit here for a cup of coffee and a good chat when a friend stops over?

If there are pieces of furniture you want moved out of the room or into the room, do that first. Once your furniture is appropriately positioned, you are ready to begin. This shouldn't be too hard a room to do, so keep going and you should breeze through it.

Tabletops and Sofas

Empty everything off the coffee table and end tables into three piles: keep, store elsewhere, or toss. Leave at least two-thirds of each coffee table and end table clear. Rotate some interesting items as a display that will be a conversation starter.

Now follow the clear line of sight by dusting and polishing the tabletops in your living room. This is a good time to put away books, papers, and knickknacks that belong elsewhere. Keep only recent magazines and recycle or store the rest in a magazine holder.

Toys should be returned to the playroom or children's bedrooms. Travel brochures and papers go back in a file. Holiday decorations should be put away. China figurines should be washed and thoroughly dried before putting them back.

Clear any clutter off the sofa and fluff the pillows. Be sure to check under the seat cushions—you might find something valuable! Windows, picture frames, and glass tabletops should be cleaned as well. Soon the room should be back in pristine condition with this extra effort.

Floor

For a thorough cleaning, move the furniture and clean the floor. As you vacuum or mop, take note of any piles that may have started to accumulate, such as photos and books in a corner. You may even find something valuable you have been looking for.

Floor plants may need repotting and fertilizer. Large silk trees or plants should be dusted or replaced. This is also a great time to vacuum or wash the baseboards for an extra-clean look.

Bookshelves

As you dust the shelves, empty one shelf at a time into two piles: keep or donate. Look for any books and knickknacks you have outgrown and pass them on to free up space. Be sure to give them away within twenty-four hours.

1. Dust and Polish Tabletops
2. Organize Cabinets
3. Fine-Tune Activity Zones

SPACE-SAVING TIP #34

Practice the "two-minute pickup" every time you leave the living room and it will stay clean.

Cabinets and Closed Storage

It's amazing how valuable items can be hidden away in a drawer or on a shelf and turn into clutter over the years. That's why it's important to go through the "hidden" storage areas such as:

Chest with drawers. If you have a chest with drawers, sort the contents one drawer at a time into three piles: keep, store elsewhere, and toss. You can easily dispose of old brochures and newspaper clippings, pet toys, and children's toys that your family has outgrown. Now is the time for a fresh start in your drawers.

Desk. A small desk or writing table can be nice in the living room, but it can also attract clutter. Go through each drawer and keep only what you like and still use.

Front closet. Often near the living room is a front closet by the entryway. Clean this just like a bedroom closet: rod hanging items first, floor second, and shelving third. For more information about closet cleaning, see chapter 6.

The front closet needs hangers for guests, hangers and hooks for family coats, and baskets for mittens and sports equipment. If too much is piled on the closet floor, it is a good sign that you need to put in shelves or a bookcase to hold all the items.

This closet may be the one to hold your dining room tablecloths, table leaves, or vacuum. Place them sideways at one end so they're not the first things you see when you open your front closet. A multipurpose closet can still look good and be functional if you keep it weeded out.

SPACE-SAVING TIP #35

Organize your photos in books for the current year and display them at the holidays. Expand their usefulness by making copies so siblings and children have their own book from you.

Activity Zones

After the clutter is cleared, then it's time to fine-tune the room by activity zones. The living room may be larger than other rooms, so it often consists of more than a sofa and chairs. It can also be used for other types of activities.

Music. A piano or other musical instrument, such as an organ or guitar, in the living room can be a focal point. Arrange furniture in the room so people can easily listen to your resident musician. Also include a place for storing sheet music, such as the piano bench or antique music cabinet. A music stand for a string or band instrument player can be attractively displayed by a plant or floor lamp.

Be sure there is a place for the accompanying music case so it doesn't end up on your sofa each day. A luggage rack can hold the instrument case and an ottoman with a hinge can hold attachments and music.

Photo albums. A living room bookshelf can be a lovely place to display family photo albums. Similar size binders and leather lookalikes add a touch of class. A label maker can attractively label the spine with the year and contents. Filing your family history from oldest to newest will make it easy for family to pull a photo album off the shelf and relive chapters of your life.

It may be time to scan your pictures and save them digitally. This would be a project in itself to assign to a later date, but tackling one book per year could make this an important family legacy. This also makes it easy to divide up family photos with everyone getting equal photos.

Family heirlooms. The living room is a good place to display family treasures such as an heirloom clock or arts and crafts passed on from generations. Bookshelves can display framed family world travels or significant memorabilia from family. Display some pleasant reminders that give you a sense of family history.

We have an antique desk in our front entry carved in the late 1800s by a great-great-aunt that means the world to me. It shows what talent we had in our family tree and reminds me of my love of writing and creating at a desk.

SPACE-SAVING TIP #36

Expand the usefulness of your living room to be able to read, listen to music, or do light paperwork too.

Lighten Up and Let Go

If the traffic pattern in the living room has gotten crowded over the years, it may be time to let go of some furniture and rearrange the room.

You may want to try a consignment shop to trade good items for cash. This could include special furniture such as chairs, end tables, lamps, and art. Offer china and valuable items to relatives or sell them on eBay. You could also sell them online through a local vendor such as Craigslist to save you the time and expense of shipping.

Find a local charity that would accept your closet items such as winter clothes, sports equipment, and books. You can sell unused musical instruments to a music store or donate them to a school band. The key is to get rid of things you no longer use before they lose their value.

Living Room Checklist

_____ 1. Is my furniture attractive and usefully arranged, with all excess furniture given away?

_____ 2. Are the tabletops attractively arranged and uncluttered?

_____ 3. Do my bookshelves look nice and hold what I currently enjoy?

_____ 4. Are my cabinets and chests cleaned out and simple?

_____ 5. Are my photo books labeled and up to date?

_____ 6. Does my front closet work for me and my guests?

_____ 7. Do I have reading lamps and storage for music or desk work?

_____ 8. Are my family treasures displayed but not cluttered?

_____ 9. Is there a clear line of sight across the table tops and furniture?

_____ 10. Am I making the most of my living room so that it is useful and clutter free each day?

Tips from "The Decorating Coach," Susan Wells

Transform your living room from boring to beautiful with attention to the little details that make a big difference.

Stimulate with artwork. Pictures impart personality, but they must be the right proportion and strategically placed. Hang one or two to measure two-thirds the width of the sofa, with the bottom of the frame(s) six to ten inches above the back. A small picture will "float" on the wall, so cleverly anchor it to a grouping such as an end table and lamp. Transforms a dull corner into the center of attention!

Excite cold windows with a valance made from a spectacular fabric that adds softness and definition. Repeat the pattern with several pillows to grace the seating area. A few accents make the entire room look fresh.

Rejuvenate in a relaxing ambience by turning off the task lighting. Hide a small, inexpensive floor lamp behind a vase, plant, or small pieces of furniture, and you'll create a new look each evening.

Manage It Simply

Every home has a unique use of the living room. Make your living room an attractive space that you use, not just one you walk by every day.

- After organizing the living room for the Nelson family, I put a reading lamp from another part of the house at each end of the sofa. Immediately the room became useful for homework reading and relaxing. The parents were thrilled that their teenagers actually sat down and spent time with them as they worked at their desk in that room.

- One client noticed her baby grand piano took up a lot of space in her living room. Her kids were grown and didn't want the piano, so she sold it—to us! Our kids took piano lessons, and our oldest daughter, Christy, became a music teacher. We are grateful for this woman's willingness to let go of what wasn't useful anymore.

- Lillian's living room had always been arranged the same way. However, her daughter's friend was a decorator and repositioned the furniture and bought a new wingback chair and a matching picture to create a new setting. Many guests now enjoy Lillian's home cooking and overnight hospitality because one person shared her talents and rearranged the room to be a warmer gathering place.

Do something new in your living room space so you and your guests won't grow tired of it. And if you have family or friends with a decorating or organizing talent, accept their help when they ask!

Review: The CALM Living Room Approach

Create a Plan
○ Clear visible surfaces and polish tabletops.
○ Organize cabinets and stored items.
○ Fine-tune the room by activity zones.

Approach It by Sections
○ Keep large furniture pieces looking nice.
○ Organize special activity areas.
○ Look for hidden piles and projects and finish them.

Lighten Up and Let Go
○ Charities will pick up extra furniture and resalable items.
○ Consignment shops are good for turning items into cash.
○ Online auctions, such as eBay, are good for smaller items you can sell and ship.

Manage It Simply
Daily—Do a "two-minute pickup" to keep this room in shape.
Quarterly—Go through the front closet to keep coats and sports equipment out of the way.
Yearly—Clean the living room in the fall before holiday visitors drop by.

A well-organized living room sets the tone for an organized home. Remember to do a two-minute pickup in this space each day, and you will have a clean and usable living room for your family and guests to enjoy anytime.

You can't change anyone but you. It is your example that is going to set the tone for your home. When it is done with a loving attitude, they will take notice and start to help.

—MARLA CRILLY

13

Simplify Your Guest Room

Organizing is about making room in your life for the things that
truly matter to you. Organizing is simply creating an environment
and lifestyle that honors your priorities.

—VICKI NORRIS

The guest room . . . the spare room . . . the craft room . . . your grown child's old room . . . the computer room . . . the exercise room. Whatever you call it, it once was a bedroom that changed its purpose over the years. For this chapter we will call it the guest room and treat it as a high priority that could offer the extra space you are looking for.

The guest room often serves two or more functions, such as:

- Guest Room/Home Office
- Craft Room/Sewing Room
- Exercise Room/Guest Room
- Grown Child's Room/Computer Room

The first step in simplifying this space is to stand at the doorway and decide what purpose this room serves in your life right now. Is it for occasional overnight guests? Is it your grown daughter's childhood room that she still sleeps in when she comes to visit? Is it a holding room for a desk, overstuffed chair from the living room, and extra centerpieces you put together for the Spring Tea?

It's time to decide how this room could best serve you and your family now. In this chapter, you will walk through that process so you can make a change if you so desire. It's easy to simplify this room once you decide how you want to use it.

Create a Plan

Our goal is to reorganize and set up this space to be attractive and function well for your family.

Our plan consists of three steps:

1. Set up the room by purpose(s).
2. Redistribute excess items.
3. Pull the room together.

Simplify Your Guest Room

Motivation:
- Company is coming!
- I need space to pursue my project/hobby.
- It's time to clean it out and put it to good use.

Supplies:
- Three boxes for things to put away, donate, and sell
- Notepad and pen for "to-do next" steps
- Matching closet storage boxes and label maker

Time Estimate:
4 hours per activity area (guest space, crafts, sewing) and closet cleaning. For a big cleanup, multiply the time estimate by four.

Reward:
An organized room ready to use anytime.

Approach It by Sections

This room holds great possibilities for new space in your life. But finding it requires a purposeful plan.

Choose the activities your room needs to serve and then approach them one by one. Don't be afraid to get rid of things that were once useful but are no longer a part of your life. Brighten someone else's day (and your own) by passing things on.

Here's how to approach the room by activity and make the most of it. Focus on the aspects that meet your needs, and use the ideas in this chapter to springboard your own. There's great potential in this room.

Whatever your room, pull it together with one style and your favorite colors. If your room has unmatched furniture and plastic bins, pull it together by upgrading to real furniture, such as an armoire, freestanding cabinet, or built-in drawers and shelves.

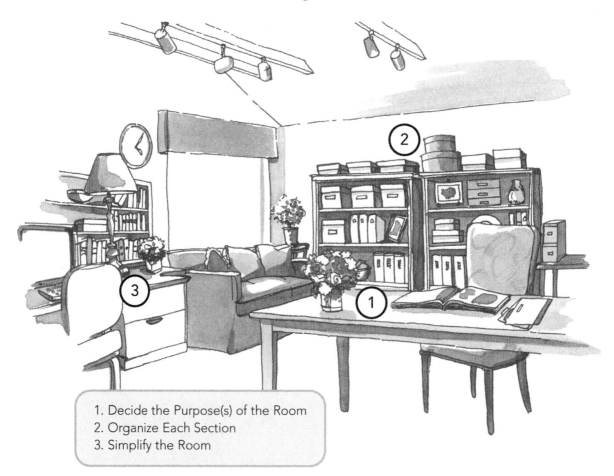

1. Decide the Purpose(s) of the Room
2. Organize Each Section
3. Simplify the Room

Guest Room

You need a few basic things to have an attractive and usable guest room. A bed with a nice bedspread, sheets, guest-ready pillows and blankets, and a place for a suitcase and hanging clothes. If your bedding consists of hand-me-downs from another room, that's perfectly fine. But if something is starting to look worn or dated, you can add it to your shopping or wish list.

Hosting overnight guests is great leverage to get things done beforehand. You may even want to freshen the room with paint or updated decorations before your next guests arrive.

In the guest room, pare down your bedding supplies to what you really use. Extra blankets and pillows can take up a lot of storage space. To simplify the room, pass on extra bedding and furniture.

It's also nice for your guests to have a reading lamp and alarm clock. Reading material, a desk, a comfortable chair, and a radio are also helpful options depending on your space—and how long you're willing for your guests to stay!

The rule of thumb for simplifying a guest room is to keep it attractive, clutter free, and tasteful.

Closet Storage

In your guest room closet, keep a section of hanging space with matching hangers for your guests, perhaps even half the closet. For personal storage in the closet, keep things neatly in matching boxes and fold items with the decorative edge forward on the shelves.

Your guest room closet will be viewed by guests, so keep it as empty as possible on the hanging bar, floor, and shelf above the hanging rod. The other half or sides of a walk-in closet could hold games, bedding, luggage, memory boxes, file cabinet, Christmas decorations, ironing board, and out-of-season clothing.

As you organize the closet, sort everything into three piles: keep, donate, or toss. Put back "keep" items in boxes with a label on the outside. If everything is stacked on the floor, measure the available closet space for shelving and either buy shelving to fit or have a closet company install shelving.

Storing your boxes on shelves makes it easier for you to retrieve a single box without unloading several boxes to get to the bottom of the pile. A well-planned closet results in easy access and more frequent use of your items.

If you need more space, add another shelf to the top of the closet. Store smaller boxes, suitcases, or memorabilia you don't need regular access to. These are items you'd like to keep and should be boxed and labeled.

SPACE-SAVING TIP #37

A room that has a single purpose, such as a guest room or craft room, is easier to set up and maintain.

Craft Room/ Sewing Room

A craft or sewing space can be a corner of a room, or it can be a dedicated room in itself. Here are some important things to remember in setting up a craft room.

Set up your worktable in the best lighting in the room, or where you feel the best. That could be directly facing a window for natural light or placed in a location you like with good lighting on the desk.

Store your craft materials by related projects. That means all the beading supplies go in one section, the fabric and sewing materials in a separate section, and knitting supplies stored in another section. Organize supplies like scissors, pens, and paper together so they are always in one location. Then you can find them no matter what project you are on.

Post a calendar with your project start and finish dates, and list what times you work on them. This time tool keeps you producing beautiful work instead of just collecting materials and puttering time away. Become a finisher by using a calendar.

A common problem in craft rooms is a hodgepodge of unlabeled plastic containers of all shapes and sizes stacked up for a temporary sense of order. Plastic containers often multiply like rabbits without a plan. A much more effective way to organize your craft space is with cabinets and drawers, whether freestanding or built-ins.

The center of your floor should be clean and the worktables clear and ready for action.

SPACE-SAVING TIP #38

Spaces that serve multiple functions should have separate areas. Do this by putting furniture in one part of the room and using another wall or corner for the other activity.

Grown Child's Room

Once your child moves out of his or her room, you have to ask yourself, "Is this room still my child's space? Do I need to keep it the same to make my child feel loved?" There are several things you can do to this room while still letting your child feel welcome.

Begin by taking pictures of the room as it is on its best day—bed made, clothes put away, etc. If you can, take a picture of your child in the room in various spots holding a favorite baseball bat or trophy. That way you have preserved the childhood memories and are freer to begin making changes. If your child has moved on to college, career, or marriage, he or she may want to see a few sentimental things on the walls, such as framed photos that have positive memories.

The dresser top and shelf collections can be gone through together in two piles: keep and give away. Encourage your child to sell current CDs and textbooks online to get some cash. Kids like that!

Binders should be labeled on the spine and papers filed. In doing so, your child may decide the papers are not worth keeping and then they can toss them.

Your goal is to place neatly labeled boxes of books, class notes, trophies, and memorabilia in the closet so they can be transferred when your child has a place of his or her own.

Home Office

In chapter 10, we looked at several ways to simplify your home office. If you have a blended guest room and home office, you need to have nice drawers and file space to meet your needs. Some guest rooms that double as home offices use a sleeper sofa with a desk and laptop. Other guest rooms use attractive shelving, a desk with drawers, and a lateral file that doubles as an end table.

SPACE-SAVING TIP #39

Organize the guest room so it is visually clean: dresser tops clear, floor clean, and storage areas organized and labeled. Keep it simple by passing on unused items.

Exercise Room

A spare room can also be used for exercise equipment. Regularly evaluate if you are using the treadmill, stationary bike, or weights. If not, what should you do? Let these items go, join a gym, and claim more space for another purpose.

Lighten Up and Let Go

The key to maintaining order is to clean up your workspace before you leave the area. If you have a craft space, then at the end of a project, cull through the materials and pass on excess materials to another crafter before the items get old and out of style.

If you have a room for overnight guests, count how many blankets and sheets you have to minimize your storage areas. You will feel good passing on extra blankets and bedding that are still good and useful to many charities.

If you have a grown child's room, make the decision now to donate or sell unused childhood toys. If a particular toy has a lot of sentimental value, you can give it to your child or take a picture of it to keep in your child's memory book.

Guest Room Checklist

_____ 1. Is the purpose for this room useful and clear?

_____ 2. Do I have everything in place for guests?

_____ 3. Is there space for guests to hang their clothes, and are my personal storage items neatly arranged and labeled?

_____ 4. Is the workspace clear and the materials stored neatly so crafts and projects are getting done?

_____ 5. Am I downscaling my child's memorabilia and changing the room to reflect his or her adulthood?

_____ 6. Is the computer set up and supplies organized?

_____ 7. Do I use my exercise equipment daily, and is it attractive and clutter free?

_____ 8. Do I always clean up the room before leaving?

_____ 9. Have I distributed all the excess furniture, bedding, and supplies?

_____ 10. Is this room clearly defined and functioning well for my family's current needs?

Tips from "The Decorating Coach," Susan Wells

A welcoming feeling will greet your weary guests when you've indulged them with quick pick-me-ups throughout the guest room. Layer crisp bed linens that flatter the wall color. Maximize the calm by draping a comfy throw that introduces new texture and tone.

The jewelry of the room can emerge from the most ordinary pieces. Grace a lampshade by gluing fanciful fringe to the edge, then repeat the embellishment along plain pillows. Accent a tissue box with a pretty cover.

Elegant touches are easily added by replacing worn-out hardware with charming, inexpensive new designs. Exchange doorknobs with ones that flatter the room's ambience. Purchase an overhead light fixture that crowns the room with charm. All in all, surround your loved ones with touches that make them feel especially pampered.

Manage It Simply

Clean up before you leave the room, and you'll rarely have to do anything but a light touch-up cleaning to keep it in tip-top shape.

- Kay occasionally had guests but could never remember if the bedsheets were clean. Sometimes she had to rewash them the day her guests arrived just to be sure. So we talked about a way to solve the problem. She agreed that the morning her guests left, she would wash the bedsheets immediately. That way, she could rest assured that her sheets were "company ready" all the time.

- Judy's husband worked from home, she homeschooled her two children, and she had a side business of making quilts. The problem was she had thirteen quilt orders for friends and her business that she never felt she had time to do.
  We counted the weeks until Christmas and found there were exactly thirteen. I coaxed her into picking realistic times to work, and she decided she could devote from 1 to 3 p.m. on Monday, Tuesday, and Thursday to complete

one quilt per week. Friday became her day to deliver or mail the quilt. Creating a plan and solving the time problem let her enjoy her hobby.

- Dora had a flair for decorating for church and business events and even had three-week classes to train others. The problem? "I have too many decorations from past events and after all these years I'm getting tired of so much," she said. "What can I do with them since they're still really good?"

  "You could offer them to your class graduates either to give away or sell them," I suggested. "Your former students are your best market."

  Dora did, and the time it took let her emotionally disengage from each set of centerpieces and displays. She was reclaiming her spare room.

Review: The CALM Guest Room Approach

Create a Plan
○ Decide on the purpose of the room.
○ Organize each section.
○ Pull the room together with color and upgrades.

Approach It by Sections
○ Set up a guest room with amenities and closet space.
○ Organize the room by activity spaces.
○ Use the closet for neatly stored personal items.

Lighten Up and Let Go
○ Donate extra bedding and clothes to a local charity.
○ Sell anything of value.
○ Give craft and sewing materials to others who would appreciate them.

Manage It Simply
Daily—Same-day cleanup keeps the room always ready.
Weekly—Complete a project on your craft calendar.
Seasonally—Go through the closet and keep it weeded out.

To find the space you never thought you had, look to rooms that are no longer bedrooms and reclaim them. You'll feel like you have a new house when you change a room's purpose to fit your current needs.

Sorting, as painful as it may be, is a critical step in organizing any area of your home. You simply can't create an organized space or system without knowing what you need to organize.

—LAURA LEIST

Simplify Your Storage Space

You're finally ready to tackle the "big" storage rooms in your home: the garage and the basement. With clear and simple guidelines, you can easily do these rooms. Plus, we will prepare you for your next move, whenever that comes. At the end of these chapters, you will feel like you have graduated—and you have. Keep going; you're almost finished!

14

Simplify Your Garage

You need to think about how you want to use your garage and how
you want it to look when you are finished with this project. In simplest terms,
you need a plan. It doesn't have to be a complex one at all, but you
need a clear vision so you will know when you have achieved success.

—BARRY IZSAK

The garage can be your friend or foe. Too much stuff and too little time to get organized may have turned your garage into a labyrinth of clutter. But one, two, or even three good weekends of sorting can give you more room, pleasant surprises of found items, and renewed interest in your hobbies.

Armed with determination and a good plan, you can park your car in the garage, safely store extra supplies in labeled boxes, and use your tools and workbench again.

So why do so many garages become filled with so much clutter? The trouble begins when you have not answered the following three important questions:

1. Whose space is it anyway?
2. What do we keep in there?
3. Who's going to clean it out?

These three issues are important to consider so you don't create an emotional explosion over a broken lawn mower, a bag of tile grout from an unfinished bathroom, or the ice cream maker you got as a wedding gift and haven't used in fifteen years.

Never fear. There are ways to get through the emotional entanglements and garage cleaning. And the benefit is always order and extra space. Put on your organizing hat and be ready to clean the garage. Today's the day!

Create a Plan

Your family's garage-organizing plan must be clear to everyone involved. Even if you are single, consider dividing the two side walls into masculine and feminine walls. An effective overall approach looks like this:

1. Garage floor
2. Main wall
3. Left wall: the "guy" wall
4. Right wall: the "gal" wall
    Bonus: Rafter storage

That means distributing items to their rightful categories to clear the center of the garage floor. Then you can deal with the surrounding three walls. (The garage door isn't considered a wall.)

You now have four clearly defined areas to organize in the garage. As you sort the items on the floor and each wall, organize by sections: trash and recycle bins, lawn and garden supplies, workshop tools, sports equipment, and household storage. Fine-tuned areas could include a personal storage box or space for each person.

Assign organizing an area to whoever uses those items most, such as sports equipment to kids, tools to Dad, and household items to Mom. What they organize, they should maintain. You may want to take a picture of how the area was before and after as reminders of your progress. If the area deteriorates, you can pull out your picture of how it should be maintained. Pictures are more motivational than any lecture.

Simplify Your Garage

Motivation:
- Our family needs to get things in order and back in their place.
- I'd like to actually park our car(s) in the garage!
- I want to stop the embarrassment of a messy garage.

Supplies:
- Index cards, tape, and markers for signs
- Notepad and pen for next steps
- Big, empty trash bins
- Plastic storage boxes with lids
- Gym shoes, snacks for breaks, and a plan

Time Estimate:

4–8 hours per section, depending on how many things you have to organize

Reward:

An organized garage that holds your cars, tools, storage items, hobbies, and outdoor activity equipment

Approach It by Sections

A garage is usually a box-shaped space, so items can easily span the perimeter of the room. If you live in snow country you will have shovels and snow blowers, while families in warmer climates may have pool equipment and beach chairs. You need to adapt your organizing categories to meet your particular needs.

Floor

To begin creating order in your garage, begin by clearing the center of the floor. If you intend to keep your car(s) in the garage every day, then you need to make sure your garage floor is no longer a dumping ground for miscellaneous clutter. It's possible.

To sort the items on your garage floor, label the walls with signs for four major categories per wall, such as:

Left Wall—The "Guy" Wall
- Yard and lawn equipment
- Workshop tools and paint
- Gardening tools
- Sports equipment

Right Wall—The "Gal" Wall

- Household storage
- Giveaway Items
- Children's toys
- Pet care supplies

Rafters—Household Storage

- Holiday decorations
- Household carpet and trim molding
- Suitcases

    (If you have no rafter storage, put these items on the left and right wall space.)

By setting up signs around the room, you can cut your sorting time in half if you decide now rather than later where things go. As you sort through your belongings in the garage, place similar items together. If there is not room along the garage walls, then place your signs along the driveway or side of the house.

In this major sort, focus on clearing the center of the floor. When you can see the center of the floor, this visible sign of progress will motivate you to keep going.

Sweep the garage floor when you can see significant space. This will make you feel like you're really cleaning the garage—plus, you won't track old dirt and grease into the house.

The initial big sort of the center of the garage floor requires decisions. Some things have to go to make room for today's activities in your life. Not everything can stay.

SPACE-SAVING TIP #40

Cardboard boxes tend to wilt over time, so upgrade your garage storage to plastic containers with lids.

Main Wall

This is often the most noticed wall of the garage from the driveway. It is usually deeper than the side walls, so it is valuable for deeper items.

Refrigerator or freezer. These need to be near an electric plug and, if they are used often, as close to the door to the house as possible.

Workbench. This may be situated at the back of the garage so you can allow room

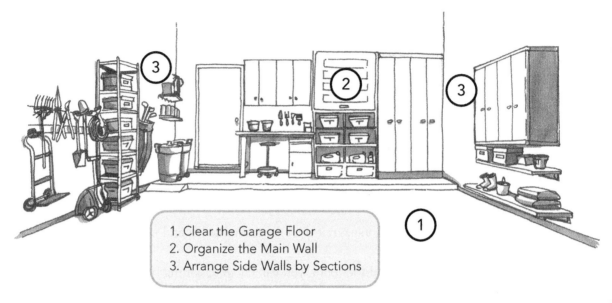

1. Clear the Garage Floor
2. Organize the Main Wall
3. Arrange Side Walls by Sections

for a stool. Be sure there is electricity for power tools and storage for related items in drawers and cabinets.

Cabinet storage and shelving. Kitchen cabinets make ideal storage over a workbench or a craft area in the back of the garage.

Washer and dryer. Depending on their size and the power connections, these may need to be on the main wall of the garage.

Give some thought to what you put on the deeper back wall of your garage. Don't put anything narrow on this wall that could go on a side wall unless you need the space for walking to your car.

The other most important space in the garage is next to the door to the house. Do you want your trash and recycle bins there so you can drop in trash from the house? Or do you want a clear ledge to set things down as you open and close the door?

SPACE-SAVING TIP #41

An important step in garage organizing is using large labels for your boxes that you can see from a distance. A black marker and index card will do the job well.

Now that the bigger items are placed on the main wall of the garage, it is time for sorting and containerizing smaller belongings. Make a diagram of what you want on each of the two remaining walls.

Left Wall: The "Guy" Wall

Here are some tips for organizing your "guy" wall or the tools for outside of the house:

- Keep yard tools on the same side so you don't have to crisscross the garage.
- Keep your most used sections the easiest to access, even with the cars parked in the garage.
- Store outdoor equipment, such as rake, edge trimmer, shovel, or broom on a hanging rack, on wall hooks, or put them in an upright can.
- Workshop tools and paint occupy anywhere from three feet to three yards of wall space, depending on the hobbyist or serious carpenter. Keep all the equipment in drawers, bins, and a pegboard over a workbench to keep this person happy and your home in good repair.
- Gardening tools should be near workshop tools because they need the same kind of drawers and shelving, even if someone else does the gardening. Keep these areas organized so more work is done.
- Sports equipment like golf clubs, tennis rackets, soccer balls, cleats, hockey gear, and bats can be propped upright in a cabinet so these items won't fall. Use bins or sports racks to hold balls and related gear.
- Hardware stores and closet companies can outfit you in modular cabinets and wall-mounted rack systems to get ladders and wheelbarrows out of the way.
- If you live in an area that gets winter freezes, do not keep aerosols or paint in the garage. If you live in a warm climate, stay away from cardboard that goes limp from humidity, and do not store items in the garage that may melt in the summer heat, such as candles and other decorations.

Right Wall: The "Gal" Wall

After the tools, yard equipment, and sports equipment are organized, it's time to sort the remaining items. Your garage's "gal" wall will likely include the following items, which relate more to inside the home:

- Storage bins on same-sized shelves that can hold a box per person, per hobby, or other household storage. Kitchen appliances that are used only once a year (such as ice cream maker or turkey roasting pan). Yearbooks and memorabilia, though these are best stored in the house. As long as items are still useful or important, you can keep them inside if you have the space.

- Children's toys and "keep" items sometimes need a place beyond their bedroom. Put them in labeled boxes so they don't become a clutter heap on the floor.
- Pet care takes space, so put together all leashes, cages, terrestrial cages, and supplies. Pass on what could be used by someone else.
- Donation boxes are important to have permanently in the garage so you can drop items in there for charity all year long. Mark three boxes—"Giveaway Clothes," "Giveaway Household Items," and "Giveaway Media."

Rafter Storage

Ceiling supports or rafters can expand your storage space in the garage. These can be made out of plywood and hung above the garage door or over the front hood of the car. Make your own, or purchase a professional system if you plan to stay in your home more than two years.

Ceiling shelving can hold the following:

- Holiday decorations stored in plastic bins.
- Luggage stored on ceiling-suspended supports.
- Patio umbrellas and picnic chairs stored out of the way on upper shelving.

 SPACE-SAVING TIP #42

Simplify the look of your garage by choosing the same kind of containers, either solid or see through, and neatly labeling the contents.

Lighten Up and Let Go

Once you organize your garage, you should have a lot to get rid of. Take these items away the same day to a charity or dump to complete your task successfully.

Be sure to get your money's worth out of your weekly garbage and recycle pickups by emptying all the household wastebaskets. Remember, clean homes have one thing in common—empty wastebaskets—because they pay attention to the little details.

Now go back and review your garage with this checklist.

Garage Checklist

____ 1. Is the garage floor clear in the center and cars able to fit?

____ 2. Is the main wall attractive and items intentionally well placed?

____ 3. Are all the yard and workshop tools in one area?

____ 4. Are all the storage boxes in one area and labeled?

____ 5. Are items placed in clearly defined sections?

____ 6. Are all containers labeled and able to withstand temperature changes?

____ 7. Have the ceiling storage items been labeled and sorted?

____ 8. Are the trash and recycle bins easy to open and use?

____ 9. Do I empty the house wastebaskets for weekly pickups?

____ 10. Does the garage function well for storage, yard items, and recreational purposes?

Tips from "The Decorating Coach," Susan Wells

A garage need not look dingy. Painting the doors will add points of visual interest, as well as mask the scuff marks. Repeat the color beneath with "floor and porch" paint.

A tent-flap tarp will hide unsightly items on the open shelving. Cut a piece of canvas down the middle and install onto the top shelf, overlapping the fabric slightly in the middle. Along the center edge of each tarp, attach a ring, with corresponding hooks installed at the outside edges. The cover will easily pull back when needed.

Bins in matching colors will complete the look. If you can't find the right shade, print out contents labels on tinted cardstock or use colored ink.

Manage It Simply

Every time you enter or leave your garage, look around to see that everything is in order. Putting things away now saves you so much time later. Keeping your garage in order is less of an ordeal if you keep it weeded out. Below are a few stories of what some clients did to simplify and manage their garage space.

- Trudy had a sofa and beautiful furniture for "staging" houses to sell. Yet when we organized the garage, she realized everything wasn't going to fit. She had to choose whether she wanted to put her van in the single car garage or rent a storage unit for her side business.

  Once she weighed the cost of storing the furniture with what she was making on staging, she decided to give up the business, sell the furniture, and continue the goal of getting her vehicle in the garage.

  Trudy and I started by sorting and clearing the entire floor. That left room to sort the three walls, starting from the top shelving down on each wall. In two afternoons and one evening, we completed her entire garage sort and reorganization. She was relieved.

- Cindy had homemade storage lining the walls of three sides of the garage, about thirty-six inches from the ceiling. We noticed a round hole every so often and realized the prior owners had cleverly used sliding closet doors as the base shelving when they replaced their closet doors with mirrored doors.

  The shelving was perfectly sized for two thirty-gallon totes to store back to back. We placed inherited family memorabilia in sealed containers in the back and often used household items in the front. A final diagram of the boxes posted in the garage and a copy kept in the house let the homeowner find anything at a moment's notice.

- David brought home cardboard boxes filled with work papers when he changed jobs. The nine boxes were meant to be temporary, but after four months they were an eyesore and showing signs of wear.

  A Saturday morning sort sitting on a three-step stool let David drop "toss" papers into a recycle box on the left and a "keep" pile on the right. Though he ended up tossing 80 percent of the papers, this was an important step for bringing closure to the prior job by reviewing all the work he had done.

  "This is hard," David said, "because I did a lot of work for that company. But I know I need to let go." And he did. I know his wife was very happy . . . because it was me!

Review: The CALM Garage Approach

Create a Plan
- ○ Clear the center garage floor.
- ○ Organize the main wall.
- ○ Arrange the two side walls.

Approach It by Sections
- ○ Organize the left wall by sections.
- ○ Organize the right wall by sections.
- ○ Organize rafters and upper shelving.

Lighten Up and Let Go
- ○ Call charities to pick up items the next week.
- ○ Hold a garage or yard sale the following weekend.
- ○ Put giveaway items on your curb with a "Free" sign.

Manage It Simply
Daily—Empty your car and break down cardboard boxes.
Weekly—Put all weekend items away by Sunday night.
Twice a year—Sweep out and go through everything.

Treat your garage like a family room—everyone uses it and everyone cleans up what they use. If you have effectively organized the garage, you will be able to spend fewer weekends cleaning the garage and more time doing your hobbies and using your tools!

So when the going gets tough, the tough get chanting; I'm making room for a new life that brings with it new opportunities. I'm not going to settle for living with junk. I deserve better! I don't care who gave that thing to me—it's gotta go.

—CHRISTOPHER LOWELL

15

Simplify Your Basement

The basement, attic, and garage are often the most disorganized rooms
in the house, because that's where we dump everything we don't want in
the living area. . . . Organizing these rooms can save time, reduce
frustration, and make household tasks easier.

—DONNA SMALLIN

By now you should be a pro at simplifying your storage areas, right? However,
you're in for your biggest challenge if you have been collecting things in your
basement. This one space itself could range from anything as simple as a washer
and dryer to multiple walled-in rooms.

The basement is like a garage in that each section can be approached in the same
way: clear the center and deal with items along each wall. Basements hold the prom-
ise of more room. And it can be fun to find useful things you've forgotten about. If it
has been awhile since you've sorted the basement, you may find plenty of things ready
to pass on and create new space. It could actually be a joy to go into your basement
once you have simplified the space.

What would you like to see happen in this space? Do you have ambitions to have
the family spend time together playing Ping-Pong, but the table is layered high with
out-of-season clothes? Do you still want to have a craft room, but the space has long
become a catchall for piles of ironing instead? It's time to reclaim that dream of family
times together or space for yourself.

Create a Plan

More than a good plan for the basement, you need a motivating deadline to sort through everything. One good deadline is that winter is coming and you want to clean it out before it is chilly down there. Or with a finished basement, it's time to clear it up so the kids can play indoors during the cold months. Another reason may be preparing a place for company to stay on the sleeper sofa.

To organize the basement, we will begin with this four-step overview:

1. Divide the organizing by section or walls.
2. Plan to sort through everything.
3. Cut contents down by one-third or one-half in each section.
4. Plan something new for the clear space.

It's so much easier to clear the basement now than later when you have to put your house up for sale (which you likely will someday). Do it now with as little pressure as possible. You make better decisions that way.

Simplify Your Basement

Motivation:
- It's time to sort through all the things in the basement.
- I need space to pursue my projects and hobby.
- Our cluttered basement is a source of tension.

Supplies:
- Signs labeled "Keep," "Donate," and "Sell"
- Notepad and pen for to-do steps
- Large trash bags
- Storage boxes with lids

Time Estimate:
2–4 hours per area.

> **Reward:**
> An organized basement that is useful and well organized.

When it comes to your basement, the problem might not be that it's unorganized but that there's just too much stuff! In this chapter, we'll look at ways to cut back and simplify the contents of this space.

Approach It by Sections

Working one section at a time creates order and gives you a sense of accomplishment. Deliver the sorted piles—keep, donate, and sell—out of the area at the end of your sorting. Sweep and vacuum to complete your work for the day.

Below are ten areas you may or may not have in your basement. They may even be in other parts of your home, so read and apply them wherever they are, or skip them if you don't have them. Start with the area that will provide the most relief and biggest results.

Wherever you work, bring in bright lighting such as a floor lamp to see the condition of each item. The extra light will keep you focused while you transform this space into a haven of organization.

Stairway

The stairway should be free of clutter. Temporarily placed things to be taken up or down the stairs are often overlooked by the people walking by. Start at the top step and work downward until each stair is empty. Be aware of walking up and down your stairs with "visual tune out" from now on. Pick things up and keep the steps clear.

Next, vacuum or sweep the steps so you won't be tracking basement dirt into your home. And if there are shelves on the stairwell wall, check each canned good, tool, or hanging item to see if you can toss or donate it. A basement stairwell should be relatively empty with good lighting. Along the stairwell walls, you can hang pictures that you want to keep but don't know where else to hang.

SPACE-SAVING TIP #43

Make an inventory list for your storage boxes in each room by numbering the box and listing its contents on an inventory sheet.

Family Area

The main area at the bottom of the stairs often is a family area for entertainment with a Ping-Pong, foosball, or pool table. This space can be well decorated or filled with your older family room furniture.

Whatever is in this family area, clean it in this fashion. The center floor area and surfaces are cleared of accumulated clutter by delivering laundry upstairs or washing it, putting decorations away, and delivering tools and sports equipment to the garage or workshop. Then work clockwise around the walls, holding each item and asking:

1. "Does this belong here or somewhere else?" Move it now.
2. "Is this part of my past that I can let go of now?" Put it in a donation box or trash bag.
3. "Is it ready to use, or do I need to fix it?" Write it on a list to repair later, or keep it where it is if it's in good, working order.

You may find things propped against the wall "temporarily" or stored in boxes. Now is the time to deal with them if you want to simplify the basement. When sorting through things, make this your motto: "Use it or lose it." This is the moment to make those decisions.

Storage Area

This could be a walled-off area or one wall of your basement. If it is a cement floor area, raise the stored boxes onto pallets to keep them away from moisture. Cardboard boxes tend to wilt in a damp basement, so upgrade to plastic containers with lids.

Empty one box at a time on a table with good lighting. Place each item into one of three piles—a "keep" pile, donation box, or a trash bag. Pull out every item to refresh your memory, even if you put it on your inventory list, and repack it. Try to whittle down the contents by one-third to one-half of what they were. Combine the remaining items in another box or find a smaller container. Label it before going on.

SPACE-SAVING TIP #44

In the basement, you may tend to use the space under well-lit areas while clutter collects in dark corners. Bring in light wherever you can to keep clutter out of dark places.

If you find items that are moldy or bug infested, toss them out. Check book pages to see that even prized books are in good shape—and consider moving them upstairs if they are.

If you can install shelving for your boxes, you will be able to pull your storage bins in and out more easily. Create a uniform look by using the same kind of containers.

If you are storing items for less than six months, you can use cardboard boxes. Beyond that time, you will want to invest in airtight boxes to protect the contents. Rotate new belongings while letting go of the old, whether crafts, tools, projects, sports equipment, or trophies.

Laundry Area

The laundry area of your basement needs good lighting so you can sort the items on the shelves along with any piled-up clothes. Bring in a lamp for now and get an electrician to rig one up overhead if need be. If your laundry space is well lit, you'll be more inclined to keep the area clean.

If you have clothes piled up, begin a load of wash as you work. Plan on thirty minutes for the wash cycle, thirty minutes to dry, and thirty minutes to fold and put it away. If you keep putting in a load and moving one out, how much time will it take you to catch up? Put a clock in the laundry area to manage your time and complete the job while you work.

As you sort your clothes piles, be sure to keep the donation box and trash bag nearby in case you find items that are no longer a part of your wardrobe. Fluff items in the dryer that need ironing and put them back in closets as well. Mending is best done upstairs. Work until the area is clean by using up all the sample detergents until your supply is a simple set. Also, see chapter 8 on simplifying your laundry space.

SPACE-SAVING TIP #45

Ask yourself, "Does this item give me more pleasure than the time and space it takes to store it?" If yes, then keep it. But if no, let it go.

Workshop

Like the "guy" wall in the garage, it's nice to have in your basement a workbench with drawers and shelves for tools and projects. The space it takes should reflect the amount of time you spend there. Little time, little space. But if this is where you like to spend your time, by all means set up this area well with everything you need.

On the other hand, if repairing or creating things in the workshop is not your favorite pastime, sort tools that could be passed on to a son-in-law or neighbor or charity to be put to use. Tools are valuable, and so is your time. Other people can use what you do not.

Desk Area

A basement can be an ideal, quiet spot to study, pay bills, or do computer work. With a desk lamp, you can stay focused in a small area.

If you set up an office in your basement, it is important that you enjoy sitting in the space or you will avoid it no matter how well it is set up. Lay out the desk space as described in chapter 10 on the home office. Now keep it clean each day. Every office needs to stay clean and organized no matter what level of the house it is in.

Children's Play Area

The children's play area requires a yearly sort (at least) because of the ages and stages kids go through with their toys. The biggest toys should be lined up on the bottom shelves or in a cabinet, and medium-size toys placed in baskets on open shelves. Your child should decide with you what stays and what goes.

If there are too many toys for your space, pack some away and rotate them in and out of a closet shelf every school vacation. Or allow your children to have a garage sale and earn some money for things they can part with. That's especially motivational once they are in grade school.

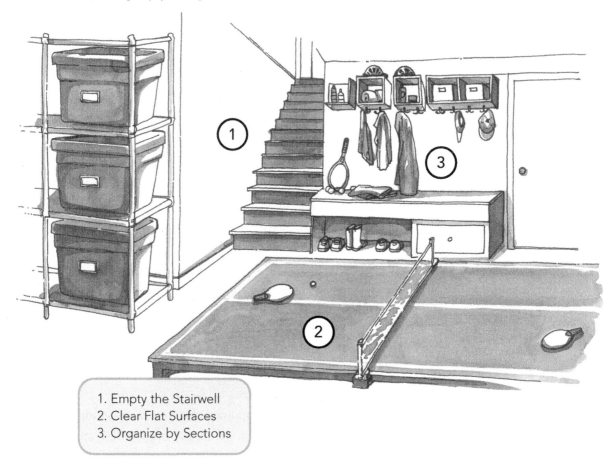

1. Empty the Stairwell
2. Clear Flat Surfaces
3. Organize by Sections

When your children are in junior high and high school, their toys become less important and they would rather have a couch, chairs, and TV to hang out in the play area. Let them fix up the area, perhaps with posters, paint, and a new rug. Making this area their own space is a good incentive for them to clear out childhood items.

But what about the toys you're not willing to part with? Instead of saving the toys for the memory of them, take a picture of your child with their favorite toys at the time they played with them. Do this yearly around their birthdays as they grow up, and watch the progression.

Exercise Area

Some basements are set up for the owner to get in shape with home exercise equipment. This equipment takes up a lot of space, but it is invaluable if you use it regularly.

If you use your exercise bike or treadmill every day, you may also want to keep a TV, DVD, or CD player nearby. If you lift weights or do floor exercises, floor mats and space to move around are important. A calendar nearby is good to track your fitness goals and chart your progress to keep you motivated.

When it comes to exercise equipment, either use it daily or sell it if you aren't motivated to use it. Think over the last six months of use and decide what you plan to do the next six months. Is exercise going to be part of your daily life? If so, keep the equipment and enjoy it. If not, sell your equipment or donate it to someone who will put it to good use.

Hobby Area

A hobby area should consist of a good worktable in a well-lit area with storage shelves and cabinets nearby. This table could be a large plywood sheet over two saw-horses for wreath making and seasonal crafts. Or it could be a sewing room with a machine and dressmaker's table.

Continually sort your project materials and keep the area neat so others will respect your time working and see your finished handiwork. Remember to not buy more materials than you use. And finish those projects you started, or donate the materials to someone who would enjoy finishing them.

Furnace Area

In older homes, a furnace heating and cooling system can be a catchall for clutter, but it is important to keep clear. Pull out, clean, sweep, and give away any items that have accumulated. Make sure everything looks in working order, and change the furnace filter. Mark the replacement date.

Add a sticker with service numbers in case the furnace goes out on a wintry night. The furnace is never as important as it is when it's not working and you're cold. But preventive maintenance is still your best defense.

Lighten Up and Let Go

Your basement can expand your living space or be a catchall that requires a major overhaul. The best way to claim space is to get rid of unused items in the basement. That way, you are putting clutter back to use at someone else's house while you free up space at your own.

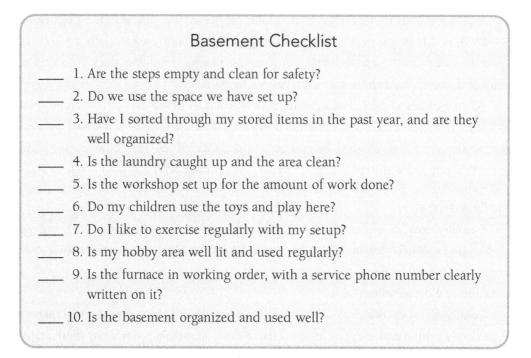

Basement Checklist

____ 1. Are the steps empty and clean for safety?

____ 2. Do we use the space we have set up?

____ 3. Have I sorted through my stored items in the past year, and are they well organized?

____ 4. Is the laundry caught up and the area clean?

____ 5. Is the workshop set up for the amount of work done?

____ 6. Do my children use the toys and play here?

____ 7. Do I like to exercise regularly with my setup?

____ 8. Is my hobby area well lit and used regularly?

____ 9. Is the furnace in working order, with a service phone number clearly written on it?

____ 10. Is the basement organized and used well?

Tips from "The Decorating Coach," Susan Wells

Rejuvenate the basement by using fixtures and quality accents that equal the decor upstairs. Control costs by gradually collecting interesting pieces from secondhand stores and flea markets.

Small windows do not have to mean small curtains. A full-length drapery will match the scale of the room and fool the eye into thinking that there is a larger window underneath. Install a decorative rod at the top of the wall and mount a drape that reaches all the way to the floor.

Unite a multipurpose room with a common theme throughout. Close off unsightly areas with a curtain installed from the ceiling. Transform an otherwise dark basement with plenty of lighting and bright accents, and it may become your favorite hideaway.

Manage It Simply

Letting go of things in the basement can be hard, but there are many benefits. Simplify your life by letting go of unused items in the largest area of your home—your basement. Build success by doing one section at a time. Toss your trash today, and deliver your excess within twenty-four hours.

- Marian was embarrassed when the sump pump overflowed in her basement while she was on vacation. Her son and his friends had to wade through the fully loaded basement and puddled water to fix it. She was mortified at her neglected housekeeping compared to the rest of her home.

   That began our twice-a-month organizing sessions to get her basement in shape. She also worked in between our sessions, tracking down appropriate places for valuables such as collectible dolls, expensive furniture, and even heirloom linens that her four children were not interested in. Over many months she emptied almost three-fourths of her basement to charity, antique collectors, and the trash. Never again would it be like that now that she took control.

- My parents filled their evenings with a hobby of pouring, painting, and firing ceramic gifts for family and business acquaintances. Everyone looked forward to their new Christmas creations, but once my parents retired, the kiln and two hundred molds were passed on to a year-round camp that gratefully received them. My parents were overjoyed to give their hobby materials to a worthy cause.

- One family thought they didn't need anything in the basement except storage. But when their son got married, they made a guest room for the newlyweds' visits and his-and-hers office space. Storage days were over. It was time to reclaim the area for guests and two home offices, which doubled the size of their living space.

Review: The CALM Basement Approach

Create a Plan
- ○ Find your personal motivation.
- ○ Clear the stairwell of accumulated items.
- ○ Plan new decorations or an activity for the cleared space.

Approach It by Sections
- ○ Divide the basement organizing by section or walls.
- ○ Plan to go through everything.
- ○ Cut contents down by one-third to one-half in each section.

Lighten Up and Let Go
- ○ Charities will accept goods from your past hobbies.
- ○ Consignment stores are good to sell your old furniture.
- ○ Antique dealers are just a phone call away.

Manage It Simply
Daily—Clean up after laundry, exercise, or games.
Quarterly—Sort through children's toys.
Yearly—Sort through your storage boxes.

Often you can donate and sell items to use toward the purchase of a new couch, exercise equipment, or updated decorations. The sky is the limit in your dreams for your basement space. Move this space beyond your past life, and simplify the contents for your present and future needs.

The top of your home—and the bottom—are danger zones, because if you have an attic or a basement, it's likely to be a haven for clutter.

—MERVYN KAUFMAN

16

Simplify Your Next Move

*Don't take everything with you. Sort through, throw out, give away,
or sell things you don't need anymore. When you've gotten to the
bare minimum—or everything you truly can't live without—start packing.*

—ILYCE R. GLINK

The day will come when it's time to move—and you can get excited that you *really* have the opportunity to go through everything you own!

When you put your house on the market, you will attract more buyers without excess belongings. Also, you have less to pack and will save money moving. And you will have less setup time at the other end before you begin your new life. It's a win-win situation all the way around—if you get busy when you hear those words, "We're moving!"

Most moving tip sheets tell you to "simply let go of the clutter." That one sentence alone may start hours of haphazard activity that ends up being frustrating and unproductive. No more! In this chapter, you will learn how to prepare for a move and set up at the other end.

This is the time to make those hard decisions and let things go. Ask yourself, "Is this item part of my past or my future?" If it's sentimental, take a picture and let it go! Save the memory in a picture, but not on your shelf.

Here's my best tip for preparing for a move: get rid of anything you don't like or use. Especially leave anything with bad memories—the bigger, the better! Whether it is an old couch, an attic full of who knows what, or a back closet full of old jackets and tools, it's time to give these things away.

Don't spend the time or money to move anything you don't like or love. Now is the time to let go of things that have been taking up space in your life. Simplify your move to make your next home easier to manage.

Create a Plan

In this chapter, you will learn how to set up to move—whether the move is for you or for a friend or relative. Very few people live in the same place forever. So when it's time to move, enjoy the opportunity to do a thorough purge of your belongings.

If you know where you are moving to, make a diagram of the rooms you will have. Then match them room by room to your current situation. It's very likely that you won't have the same number of rooms.

If you have fewer rooms, then eliminate the contents of the rooms you have to give up—an extra bedroom, a hall closet, a set of built-in bookshelves, or a basement. The rooms you won't have in your new home are the rooms you empty first at your current home.

If you are moving to a home with more rooms, decide how to divide your furniture. It may be easy to divide a combined room, like a guest room/home office, into two rooms in the new home. Other rooms may require new furniture when you get there. But just because you have more space doesn't mean you need to take everything. You probably still need to let go of things.

Simplify Your Next Move

Motivation:
- I will save money by cutting back on the things I own.
- I've wanted to sort my things. Now is the time!
- I want my new home to be clutter free.

Supplies:
- Donation boxes

- ◘ Packing boxes
- ◘ Trash bags
- ◘ Markers and labels
- ◘ Notebook with inventory sheets
- ◘ Camera or video camera

Time Estimate:
4–8 hours per room
Note: The more drawers and cabinets a room has, the more time sorting will take.

Reward:
A sense of accomplishment that you are moving just what you want to take with you.

Getting your home ready to put on the market also doubles as a way to get ready for a move. Your efforts will have double benefits—you will sell your home faster and save on moving costs. So start the simplifying process as soon as you can!

Approach It by Sections

This time, we are going to work in reverse. Here is what needs to happen to simplify nine different areas in your home. Do one room a week, or one a day, depending on the urgency of your time frame. These simple tips for each room will embellish what you already learned in prior chapters.

Start a three-ring binder called a "moving notebook" to hold all your notes and work lists. Some tabs to include are:

Rooms (one inventory sheet per room)
To-Do (before the move)
Dreams (for my new home)

✓ DONE	#	DATE	ITEM	SELL/ DONATE WHERE?	KEEP AND MOVE

Before you begin working, videotape or photograph each room in your current home. This creates a good memory of your home to take along while it is still intact. It will remind you of wall groupings of pictures, furniture placement, and china cabinet or bookshelf contents.

Set up a giveaway table with items that anyone who stops over can take. These items will be good-bye presents to your friends without you having to sell or donate them. Your friends will appreciate the memory of times spent together with that object from you.

Kitchen, Pantry, and Papers

The kitchen should be kept clean right up until the move. You can organize a drawer or cabinet as part of dinner cleanup each evening until then. Get rid of small appliances, dishes, or containers you can live without.

When you have thoroughly sorted the cabinets, begin to pack the least used items (i.e. small appliances, large pans, extra glassware) for the move. Match plastic containers and lids and toss the mismatched ones.

Use up baked goods and perishable food in the pantry and refrigerator starting now. Give away spices and use up food in the freezer. Finish up condiments in the refrigerator.

This is a room you can do wall by wall at mealtimes each day. The kitchen will be the last room packed, but you can do it a little at a time.

Family Room

Keep your family room clutter free, and try not to stack any moving pile or boxes here. This is your place to gather and relax, so keep it clean.

However, do sort through and pack the DVDs, tapes, CDs, photo books, and toys. Lots of things from here can go in garage sale boxes or on your giveaway table.

SPACE-SAVING TIP #46

Maintain order in your regular living areas. Don't create piles for the move in the family room and kitchen.

Master Bedroom and Closet

As you get dressed each day, go through one drawer or closet section, pulling out things to donate and organizing the space. One motivation to organize your dresser drawers is that movers will carry them separately and you don't want anything falling off in the driveway in front of your neighbors!

Take one day to go through every hanger in your closet and ask, "Do I like this? Do I want it in my new location?" It's expensive to move hanging items, so be sure you are only taking what you really value. Leave the "maybe" items behind.

Now sort all your shoes, handbags, belts, scarves, sports gear, and under-the-bed items. Leave no corner unturned in sorting your closets and bedrooms.

Children's Rooms

Children find it difficult to leave familiar surroundings and friends. To prepare their items for moving, sort the closet and under the bed first.

Leave the wall hangings and visual items until they are ready to take them down. As a parent, you can model the way by doing your bedroom and the rest of the house first.

Take pictures of your children doing daily activities like studying at their desk, playing in their room, playing their sport or musical instrument, and hanging out with their best friends. Later in life, they will appreciate the photo memories of their childhood home.

SPACE-SAVING TIP #47

Accept the offers of friends to bring meals and help you pack. Cherish the extra time together.

Bathrooms and Laundry Room

Now is the time to really simplify the contents of your bathrooms and laundry room. Open the cabinets in these spaces as if you were a prospective buyer. Keep the front four inches of every cabinet and shelf clear and toss all the expired or unused bottles, medications, and toiletries.

For the move, keep matched sets of towels, but demote older ones to rags to use for the move. You will need plenty of rags for cleaning when you are preparing for a move.

Once you weed through all the bathrooms, treat yourself to a cleaning service to make the rooms sparkle. Then keep these rooms as clean as possible so a buyer assumes you take care of the rest of your house this meticulously.

Home Office

You will love or hate your move depending upon the degree to which you've organized your office(s) for moving. There is nothing worse than not being able to find your checkbook, bills to pay, or current projects. Showing up with boxes marked only as "Office Papers" can seriously handicap your effectiveness on the job. Something important may not surface until three months later!

The secret to organizing your office for the move is to pack it yourself. Put everything in a file drawer, desk drawer, or box that you personally label. That way when you unpack, you will easily find your desk and contents transported just as you left them.

It takes time to sort through an office, so begin with the closet and shelving away from the desk. There you will find books, office equipment, and supplies you can take with you or give away. The more you give away now, the happier you'll be to quickly set up your office essentials and jump back into the "driver's seat" of your work life at the other end.

Be sure to sort current files and project files daily so they are complete and at your fingertips in file drawers. Make sure every loose paper on your desk ends up in a labeled file or binder before you pack.

 SPACE-SAVING TIP #48
Don't pay to move anything you don't love!

By now, you are probably in the "divide and conquer" mode of assigning people to sort the remaining rooms, based on who uses them the most.

Dining Room and Living Room

The biggest challenge in the dining room and living room is wrapping china and valuable items. Be sure to go through each item to decide if you still want it. The best advice is to downscale one-third to one-half of what you move. This gives you the feeling of a fresh start and helps you focus on your favorites.

Where do you get rid of fine items like stemware and china, or larger items like furniture or a piano? Try consignment shops, antique dealers, or estate sales. You probably could recoup some money from your nicer things in these rooms.

SPACE-SAVING TIP #49

Cherish your home and past experiences, but don't cling to them. Know the difference so you can move not only physically, but emotionally as well.

Garage and Basement

Though it may be hard to imagine, every item must come out of your garage and basement and be transported to your new location, sold at a garage sale, or given away. That can be a daunting task, but it is really just a series of small tasks together.

1. Downscale to Fit Your New Home
2. Donate and Toss
3. Label Boxes with New Room Location

Begin by setting up signs around the perimeter of the garage and basement for items to keep, sell, donate, and toss. Put boxes under each sign and begin sorting in similar sections: all the storage boxes first, the seasonal items next, and finally the currently used items.

If you put these sections away from the main walking areas, then buyers will understand that you have neatly boxed items on the far wall or corner you are moving. Or better yet, cover them with a sheet. Clean up and clear out the garage and basement so you can stack boxes from elsewhere in the house that are ready to be moved.

While you continue your sort for the move, potential buyers will be looking for the general appearance of the garage and basement, general condition of the rooms, and how their own things will fit. The more clean space you can display, the better they will like your home.

Attic, Shed, and Storage Unit

An upcoming move is the perfect time to purge an attic of all the contents that have been sitting unused over the years you've been in your current home. This is the time to dust things off, part with the old, and prepare for the new.

A shed often has accumulated overflow storage or garden equipment that may not be needed in your new home. Give these items to a neighbor or relative. Take what you will need, but not more than you will use.

A storage unit can mount up expensive monthly fees, so use this time to decide what goes with you. Often folks pick the best items to go with them and then donate the whole unit to a charity or community garage sale—if the charity will empty the rest of the unit. Many times, the expense of storing items is more than replacing the contents.

Decide now whether to continue to store your items or to downscale the whole unit and save yourself the time and expense to decide later.

Lighten Up and Let Go

Here are seven ways for you to get rid of extra things before your next move:

1. Return borrowed things like tools, books, and casserole dishes.
2. Donate usable items to charities.
3. Offer things to friends by placing them on a giveaway table in your home.

4. Offer sentimental items, like china and furniture, to grown children or other relatives.

5. Donate larger items to an auction for a tax writeoff.

6. Hold a garage sale and use the income for something new like updated bedspreads or furniture in your new home.

7. Toss or recycle it. Sometimes you have to admit that some things really are junk!

Your Next Move Checklist

_____ 1. Am I keeping the kitchen clean while I sort one shelf or drawer a day?

_____ 2. Have I sorted DVDs, tapes, CDs, and photos?

_____ 3. Am I willing to keep what I like and use in the bedroom while giving away excess closet items and bedding?

_____ 4. Do I need help filing papers and projects to prepare my home office for this move?

_____ 5. Are my bathroom and laundry belongings simplified to just the necessities?

_____ 6. Have I downscaled my dining and living room belongings to my treasured possessions?

_____ 7. If I were shopping for a house, would I like my garage and basement?

_____ 8. Are there things in my attic or storage shed that I can give away today to free up space?

_____ 9. Am I willing to box, pay to move, and unload all the items I have?

_____ 10. Am I doing something every day before I move to make it easier on myself at the other end?

Tips from "The Decorating Coach," Susan Wells

Seize the opportunity to reinvent yourself with a fresh decorating style. Only keep decor that will complement your new look. Give away supplies for the hobbies or crafts that you no longer use.

Victorian accents may not go with your new contemporary furniture, but some sentimental items can be re-invented for special occasions. Tip: your grand-mother's doilies could be used as a fanciful wrap over napkins at ladies' tea times.

A striking vase or picture frame may not match your new colors, but otherwise their shape or definition is up to date. If it doesn't walk, you can paint it! Create an upscale look with a decorative spray paint to refinish special pieces.

Manage It Simply

When you get stuck making decisions, try to keep in mind that all your things are just that—things. Say your good-byes, pack up your favorites, and move forward. Manage the move simply by keeping all your notes in a moving notebook.

- Our new neighbors moved in with a positive attitude and eagerness to meet and greet new friends. They came to the Christmas Open House where we all gathered. But the next year, they sadly reported they would be moving again . . . and many of their prior moving boxes were still packed in the garage untouched.

  Should they move those boxes again? They decided since they hadn't opened them in the entire year since their move, they would give them away. After opening each box just to be sure, they only pulled out their college yearbooks and let the rest go. Out of sight and out of mind for a year or more generally means that you can live without it.

- My friend Polly prepared to move overseas while preparing her home for renters for the years away. Organizing her home office became the top priority for privacy.

  We went through every file, loose paper, and four-drawer file cabinet. We created a complete listing of which files were in each file drawer. The files were moved and locked in the basement.

  One day she faxed me from Taiwan to pull certain files and send her information. With her file inventory, she told me exactly which drawer and what file to gather. Now that's organized when you can pull a file from overseas!

- Downscaling a parent to smaller living quarters can be difficult because of the many familiar family items involved. My brother and I and our spouses had four days to dismantle my mother's apartment and move her into half of a retirement room. We divided up the two bedrooms, kitchen, and living room.

My brother did the books, files, and my father's closet, my sister-in-law did the kitchen and pantry, and my husband did the electronic items. I arranged for antique dealers for the china cabinets, and we all staged the living room for a moving sale on the third day. On the fourth day we delivered the remainders to a charity and bags of clothes went to the Salvation Army. Together, we said good-bye to an era. It was a bittersweet memory of our good family heritage while helping a parent age gracefully.

Our mother was comforted when surrounded by her favorite afghan, family pictures, bedspread, and table decorations. You really need less than you think!

Review: The CALM Next Move Approach

Create a Plan
○ Start with a "moving notebook" to contain all your lists and plans.
○ Take pictures before you start to dismantle your home.
○ Picture clear rooms and boxes neatly stacked to go.

Approach It by Sections
○ Keep the kitchen and family room clear of boxes and clutter.
○ Sort and box up storage areas right away.
○ Label every box and area you sort to stay organized.

Lighten Up and Let Go
○ Donate and give away as much as you can.
○ Sell online or in a garage sale any items that have maintained value.
○ Let go of things that others could better use.

Manage It Simply
○ Keep your family first in the move.
○ Simplify your possessions so you can focus on people.
○ Determine to simplify yearly so you won't have as much accumulated next time.

Though many things are out of your control when you move, you can be in charge of your possessions . . . dividing them up to sell or donate and boxing up what you want to keep. Expect surprises and changes in plans. But do yourself the favor of being in control of your remaining items and free yourself of the rest. Simplify your life by moving on without the excess.

It is stressful to pack and unpack our lives, for during the process,
we relive the memories attached to our possessions.

—SUSAN MILLER

17

Simply Maintain and Multiply Your Success

An uncluttered house looks cleaner than a clean house that's cluttered.

—JUDY WARMINGTON

Congratulations! You have made it this far in simplifying your house room by room. Good for you! You are well on your way to surrounding yourself with a more simplified space.

It's important to maintain what you've accomplished. Now is a good time to take your home to the next level by learning how to manage it simply. It's really easier than you think with some planning on your monthly calendar. Doing a few small tasks each month saves you from having to do another big cleanup of your home.

Create a Plan

Staying organized comes down to recognizing where you are in the PUSH sequence, a concept I introduced in my book *Simplify Your Life: Get Organized and Stay That Way!* The PUSH sequence is a three-step process that involves you, your time, and your lifestyle. The good news is we have completed the first three of the four letters in the system.

The PUSH Sequence

Project = A one-time planned organizing and simplifying event
"YOU" = Ways for your organizing to fit your personality, so it will be easier for you to maintain
System = A dependable plan to maintain your simplifying systems
Habit = A personal routine you practice every day

Once you have established good habits, you will develop an eye for improving other systems. And oddly enough, the more simple systems you develop, the easier your life will be.

A daily system will keep most of the clutter at bay. For instance, if you wash the dishes after each meal, your kitchen will stay clean. If you put away laundry the same day, you will always have clean clothes. If you create appropriate files for your paperwork, you will have an organized desk.

Simply Maintain and Multiply Your Success

Motivation:
- I want to stay organized.
- I want to be realistic and keep up my belongings.
- I want to see this take less and less time.

Supplies:
- Index cards to make some reminder charts

Time Estimate:
15 minutes a day or 2 hours weekly

Reward:
An organized home space that is uncluttered and easy to maintain.

Let's take a look at some broader systems that can help you maintain your organized space while letting you keep simplifying your space. It truly is possible to feel confident to handle a pile of clutter and to find the time to deal with it.

Approach It by Sections

Now that you are visually attuned to your home, it's important that you don't spend all your day cleaning up. While I believe straightening up your space should be a part of your day, it should definitely not take the entire day.

Get a routine going and include the things you might not do automatically. Once these small tasks become routine, you don't need to mark them down.

Weekly Progress

Here's a sample weekly chart for you to adapt to maintain the busiest room in your house: the kitchen. Now, your kitchen doesn't need to be perfect all the time, but it won't get completely out of control if you have a system to maintain it.

The easiest step is to clean up after each meal. Beyond that you might try a schedule something like this:

Kitchen Routine—1 Week

MONDAY	TUESDAY	WEDNESDAY	THURSDAY	FRIDAY	SATURDAY	SUNDAY
Plan menus for the week	Empty household garbage	Organize one shelf (refrigerator, pantry, cabinet)	Wash the floor	Grocery shop	X	X
Spend 20 minutes each day handling the mail						(None!)

SPACE-SAVING TIP #50

Develop good organizational habits by doing things at the same time of the day and shortening the time it takes to do them.

Likewise at your desk at home or work, create a weekly system to make sure you get everything done at a reasonable pace. First, list the five things you need to do regularly (beyond mail and e-mail), and then slot them into days. Do these things Monday through Friday and take a break on the weekend.

Office Routine—1 Week

MONDAY	TUESDAY	WEDNESDAY	THURSDAY	FRIDAY	SATURDAY	SUNDAY
Send weekly team goals	Send agenda for weekly meeting	Lead weekly meeting and forecasting	Do weekly and online transfers	Submit expense report	X	X
Spend 30–60 minutes a day handling e-mails, phone calls, and paperwork.					X	X

Weekend Progress

Some tasks and space upkeep are one-time projects (like organizing bookshelves or CDs) while others are once-a-month items (like yard work or washing the car). Include them on your monthly calendar by penciling in the next three weekends with things you'd like to do.

For instance, you could spend one weekend doing yard work and the next weekend washing the car. If you want to get away for the weekend, plan to do both yard work and car washing on the same weekend so you can get away the following weekend.

Time is on your side. Maintenance of your home, yard, and car always costs less in time than repairs—and usually in money too. Keep up on those weekend projects.

Weekend Projects—4 Weekends

	Saturday/ Sunday
1st Weekend	Cut grass/shovel snow
2nd Weekend	Change oil/fix car
3rd Weekend	Wash and vacuum car(s)
4th Weekend	Clean up one part of garage

Monthly Progress

The same idea works for projects that can be done monthly. For example, everyone wants to know how to organize family photos, when the real question is, "When will I have the time?" You could make it a one-month project beginning with your current year's photos. You don't have to do your entire lifetime of photos at one time.

Start with the time and photos you currently have so you can feel a sense of accomplishment and get the systems in order. Setting up a system is a good use of your time now and for future storage.

Organize Your Photos—1 Month

	Saturday/ Sunday
1st Weekend	Gather all your photos by year in boxes
2nd Weekend	Label dates and put in photo books
3rd Weekend	Scan best photos for a digital show
4th Weekend	Scrapbook photos for birthday celebration

Do the same for your CDs by listing that as your project for the month. That way, you can slip in the time in an evening or on a weekend to sort your CDs, DVDs, or VHS tapes. It's so freeing to review what you have and get your media in order to use more.

Organize Your Media—1 Month

	Saturday/ Sunday
1st Weekend	Gather all your CDs by year in one place
2nd Weekend	Categorize by types
3rd Weekend	Divide the CDs into keep or go
4th Weekend	Alphabetize by category and put away

SPACE-SAVING TIP #51

If you live with a pack rat, agree that common spaces in your home must be clean: visible table space, counters, and furniture. Allow separate space for each person to relax and call his or her own.

Yearly Progress

The more often you go through rooms, the less time it takes. It's like sorting miscellaneous glasses and silverware in the kitchen—your cabinets and drawers keep that "simple space" look by keeping all the odd pieces out.

Your rooms are the same way. The more often you sort through them, the more likely they are to stay organized and the less time it takes to maintain them. Here's a sample yearly calendar for maintaining your space:

January—Bedrooms and closets	July—Vacation
February—Kitchen and recipes	August—Children's rooms
March—Files and taxes	September—Decorating
April—Yard and garden	October—Photo books
May—Garage and cars	November—Media and holiday preparations
June—Children's papers	December—Enjoy the holidays

SPACE-SAVING TIP #52

Decide how much you want to cut back when you sort out a space, say by one-half. This target will help you decide whether to keep something or let it go.

Lighten Up and Let Go

The key to keeping up your space is to schedule regular charity pickups and deliveries. I recommend every quarter if you want to keep the clutter at bay.

The benefits are new space and a tax deduction, more space and cash in hand, and personal enjoyment, plus compliments from other people. It's a win-win all the way around.

Maintenance Checklist

_____ 1. Are all the areas working well that I need?

_____ 2. Is there a clear line of sight in any room I walk into?

_____ 3. Are my personal spaces looking good and relaxing for me?

_____ 4. Are the rooms with daily activity picked up by the end of the day?

_____ 5. Are the more formal rooms uncluttered and welcoming?

_____ 6. Are my storage areas minimized and labeled to meet our needs?

_____ 7. Do I have a sorting project scheduled soon?

____ 8. Do I have a plan for how to stay organized?

____ 9. Do I have regular outlets to give away my excess things?

____ 10. Do I enjoy my home and possessions as they are now?

Tips from "The Decorating Coach," Susan Wells

Will the decorating ever end? Not really. Contentedness is the key to enjoying what you have, but at the same time, stay on a learning curve. If you can't create, then simply re-create your home with ideas from inspiring designers.

Visit homebuilders' model homes to learn design principles. Clip pictures from magazines and visit Web sites for free tips. Collect ideas in a binder, then categorize by topics of interest, such as rooms, colors, and furniture.

Acquire top-quality accessories at discount prices by watching for good sales. Divide your decorating projects into reasonable time frames, and you'll keep your enthusiasm up. Swap your skills with a friend, and together you'll tackle projects you never would have on your own.

Manage It Simply

You can keep your simplified space if you become aware of the habits that help or hinder your accumulation tendencies.

If you are an "organized saver," you will have to visit a charity drop-off several times a year to keep that habit under control.

If you love ideas and books, you will have to continually weed your file drawers and bookcases to stay within their confines.

If you're always on the go, you will need quick but productive systems to keep up on your daily mail, laundry, and household pickups.

A simplified home creates a sense of serenity and order. Every clear countertop and organized piece of mail helps you feel good about yourself and your space. Every small victory counts in the overall goal of simplifying your space. These are habits you can learn and succeed at.

Review: The CALM Maintenance Approach

Create a Plan
- ○ Weekly routines will help you maintain what you've done.
- ○ Weekends will give you a boost on household projects.
- ○ Monthly calendar goals by room will make it easy.

Approach It by Sections
- ○ One drawer, shelf, or cabinet at a time
- ○ One room at a time
- ○ One section of your home and office will get you there

Lighten Up and Let Go
- ○ Donate items to your favorite charity.
- ○ Sell items in the classifieds or online to gain space and cash.
- ○ Family and friends often appreciate donations.

Manage It Simply
- ○ Regular maintenance is always easier than a big cleanup.
- ○ Multiply your success by improving your simplifying skills.
- ○ Keep asking yourself, "How can I do this more easily?"

Every step counts toward your overall goal of simplifying your space. Too much "stuff" can leave you bogged down and depressed. But when you change your space, you change your life. A new life of order and freedom is ready for the taking as you simplify your space!

The more stuff you have, the more stuff you have to take care of and the more space you need to store it. Make a conscious decision to let someone else take over the caretaking.

—DONNA SMALLIN

Acknowledgments

A creative book like this takes a team of people, and I was blessed to have the best! Debbie Wickwire, acquisitions editor, saw the vision clearly from the beginning for this "successful" book along with the first two books with W Publishing Group, now Thomas Nelson. Thank you, Debbie, the marketing team, and Thomas Nelson Publishing House for believing in me and these three books. You have been a joy to work with in this endeavor.

The partnership with Women of Faith's LifeStyle line of products has brought me new friends I love, including every one of the speakers and staff! I even moved closer to headquarters in Dallas because I like you gals so much.

This book had the outstanding feature of Sabra Inzer's artwork, which helped us diagram the concepts so beautifully. You're a pro, Sabra, at making my words come alive through visuals. Thank you so much.

Decorating Coach Susan Wells, professional redesigner, stager, and speaker, helped us "tie the bow on the ribbon" with decorating tips at the end of each chapter.

Special thanks to editor Jennifer Stair, who shaped the manuscript with her grammatical eye and good common sense. Thanks, Jennifer. You're a true expert with communicating through the printed word.

Lee Hough and Alive Communications, thank you for arranging three books in the Simplify for Success series: *Simplify Your Life, Simplify Your Time,* and *Simplify Your Space.* We celebrate again.

My personal thanks goes to my audiences and clients since 1985 who have been generous and enthusiastic with their responses! Thank you for allowing me into your lives.

My network of family, friends, my e-mail prayer team, San Diego Christian Writing group members, and AWSA friends have made the past seven years a wonderful writing journey. Who says you can't learn something new in midlife? I'm glad for each of you encouraging me and cheering me onward.

I thank God for the blessings of creativity and the gift of making complicated things easier for people. Not only did God answer my prayer to help me get organized years ago, but He made me a messenger of hope to this generation of busy people. No generation before has seen so many demands on their time. I am glad to be part of the solution to everyday problems.

Finally, I want to acknowledge you, my reading friend, for your courage to make changes in your life. "The Decorating Coach," Susan Wells, and I have taken the book a step further and included photos of the chapter concepts at our Web sites: www.OrganizingPro.com and www.TheDecoratingCoach.com. Visit us often as you simplify your space.

Recommended Resources

Home Organizing Books

Aslett, Don. *Clutter's Last Stand*. Cincinnati, OH: Writers Digest, 1984.

Bouknight, Joanne Keller and John Loecke. *Home Organizing Idea Book*. Newtown, CT: The Taunton Press, 2006.

Crilly, Marla. *Sink Reflections*. New York: Bantam Books, 2002.

Empson, Lila. *Simple Living for Busy People*. Grand Rapids: Inspirio, 2004.

Glovinsky, Cindy. *Making Peace with the Things in Your Life*. New York: St. Martins, 2002.

Izsak, Barry. *Organize Your Garage in No Time*. Indianapolis: Que, 2005.

Kaufman, Mervyn. *Quick! Clutter Free*. New York: American Media Mini Mags, 2005.

McNulty, Tom. *Clean Like a Man*. New York: Three Rivers, 2004.

Morgenstern, Julie and Jessi Morgenstern-Colon. *Organizing from the Inside Out for Teens*. New York: Owl, 2002.

Morgenstern, Julie. *Organizing from the Inside Out*. New York: Henry Holt, 1998.

Ordesky, Maxine. *The Complete Home Organizer*. New York: Friedman Group, 1993.

Schechter, Harriet. *Let Go of Clutter*. New York: McGraw-Hill, 2001.

Starr, Meryl. *Home Organizing Workbook*. San Francisco: Chronicle, 2004.

Stoddard, Alexandria. *Creating a Beautiful Home*. New York: Avon, 1993.

General Organizing Books

Barnes, Emilie. *Survival for Busy Women*. Eugene, OR: Harvest House, 2002.

Berry, Joy. *What to Do When Your Mom or Dad Says . . . CLEAN YOUR ROOM!* New York: Grolier, 1981.

Felton, Sandra. *The Messies Manual*. Old Tappan, NJ: Revell, 2005.

Felton, Sandra. *When You Live with a Messie*. Grand Rapids: Revell, a division of Baker Publishing Group, 2004.

Kendall-Tackett, Kathleen. *The Well Ordered Home*. Oakland, CA: New Harbinger Publications, 2003.

Knight, Porter. *Organized to Last*. Shoreham, VT: Discover Writing Press, 2005.
www.discoverwriting.com.

Leist, Laura. *Eliminate Chaos*. Seattle: Sasquatch, 2006.

Lowell, Christopher. *Seven Layers of Organization*. New York: Clarkson/Potter, 2005.

Mission: Organization. Des Moines, IA: Meredith, 2004.

Norris, Vicki. *Restoring Order*. Eugene, OR: Harvest House, 2006. Used by permission, www.harvesthousepublishers.com.

Silver, Susan. *Organized to Be the Best: Transforming How You Work,* Fifth Edition, Los Angeles: Adams Hall, 1989–2006, www.adams-hall.com.

Smallin, Donna. *Organizing Plain and Simple*. North Adams, MA: Storey, 2002.

Walsh, Peter. *How to Organize Just About Everything*. New York: Free Press, 2004.

Online Auctions and Sales

eBay (Auction Drop, QuickDrop, and iSold It will manage your eBay sale for a fee)

Buyselltrades.com

Yahoo Auctions

uBid.com

OnSale.com

Craigslist

(Note: To calculate the value of your donations, consult the Internal Revenue Service publication 561, "Determining the Value of Donated Property," available at www.irs.gov.)

Freebies

www.craigslist.org (post under "free")

www.freecycle.org

www.excessaccess.com

A professional waste remover (listed under "garbage removal" in the telephone book)

"Free" sign at your curb on the weekend

Charities for Donations

www.SalvationArmy.org

www.Goodwill.org

www.pcsforschools.org

www.techsoup.org/recycle

www.worldcomputerexchange.org

Organizing Websites

Judy Warmington, Woman Time Management (womantimemanagement.com), Hudsonville, MI. womantimemanagement@comcast.net

Maria Gracia of www.GetOrganizedNow.com

About the Author

MARCIA RAMSLAND, professional organizer, international speaker, and author, is well known as "The Organizing Pro" for her practical skills and tips to manage busy lives. She is a sought-after speaker and media personality appearing on radio, TV, and national magazines such as *Real Simple, Woman's Day,* and *Better Homes and Gardens.*

Marcia believes everyone can become better organized and simplify their lives with the right teaching and tools. She has helped hundreds of clients and audience participants conquer organizing issues across the country. Marcia recently reorganized the spaces in her home by relocating from San Diego to Dallas.

For the Organizing Pro's Free Ezine or contacting Marcia, go to
www.OrganizingPro.com or Simplify@OrganizingPro.com.

Other Books by Marcia Ramsland

Ages and Stages of Getting Children Organized. San Diego: Kirkland, 2006.
Simplify Your Life: Get Organized and Stay That Way! Nashville: W Publishing Group, 2004.
Simplify Your Time: Stop Running and Start Living! Nashville: W Publishing Group, 2006.

WOMEN OF FAITH®

Women of Faith, North America's largest women's conference, is an experience like no other. Thousands of women — all ages, sizes, and backgrounds — come together in arenas for a weekend of love and laughter, stories and encouragement, drama, music, and more. The message is simple. The result is life-changing.

What this conference did for me was to show me how to celebrate being a woman, mother, daughter, grandmother, sister or friend.
— Anne, Corona, CA

I appreciate how genuine each speaker was and that they were open and honest about stories in their life   even the difficult ones.
— Amy, Fort Worth, TX

GO, you MUST go. The Women of Faith team is wonderful, uplifting, funny, blessed. Don t miss out on a chance to have your life changed by this incredible experience.
— Susan, Hartford, CT

The wise woman builds her house, but with her own hands the foolish one tears hers down.

—PROVERBS 14:1

CPSIA information can be obtained at www.ICGtesting.com
Printed in the USA
LVOW03s1941100114

368864LV00002B/7/P